PRASNA TANTRA

Prasna Tantra

BANGALORE VENKATA RAMAN

GAYATRI DEVI VASUDEV

MOTILAL BANARSIDASS
INTERNATIONAL
DELHI

Reprint Edition : Delhi, 2025
Eighteenth Reprint : 2013
First Edition : 1969

© MOTILAL BANARSIDASS INTERNATIONAL
All Rights Reserved

ISBN : 978-81-19394-74-6 (PB)
ISBN : 978-81-19394-82-1 (HB)

Also available at
MOTILAL BANARSIDASS INTERNATIONAL
H.O. : 41 U.A. Bungalow Road, (Back Lane)Jawahar Nagar, Delhi - 110 007
4261 (basement) Lane #3,Ansari Road, Darya Ganj, New Delhi - 110 002
203 Royapettah High Road, Mylapore, Chennai - 600 004
12/1A, 2nd Floor, Bankim Chatterjee Street, Kolkata - 700 073
Stockist : Motilal Books, Ashok Rajpath, Near Kali Mandir, Patna - 800 004

No part of this book may be reproduced in any form or by any electronic or mechanical means including information storage and retrieval systems without permission in writing from the publishers, excepts by a reviewer who may quote brief passages in a review.

Printed in India
MOTILAL BANARSIDASS INTERNATIONAL

Contents

Preface .... *(ix)*
General Introduction .... *(xi)*
Chapter 1: Uses of Horary Astrology 1
    How to Put A Query? 2
    The True Astrologer 2
    About the Querist 3
    Answering More Than One Query 5
    Planetary Avasthas 6
    Results of Avasthas 6
    Planetary Indications 7
    Events to Know from Different Houses 11
Chapter 2: Bhava Prasna 14
    General Estimate 14
    Success of Object in View 15
    Malefic Combinations 18
    First House Questions 20
    Second House Questions 23
    Third House Questions 27
    Fourth House Queries 30
    Fifth House Questions 34
    Sixth House Questions 41
    Employer-Employee Relations 49

Seventh House Questions 51
Eighth House Questions 62
Ninth House Questions.. 66
Tenth House Questions.. 72
On Realising the Object... 75
Questions Pertaining to the Eleventh House 80
Twelfth House Questions 86

Chapter 3: On Special Questions 88
Return of a Person in Exile 88
Missing Person: Alive or Dead?............................. 91
Whether the Traveller is Alive or Dead 98
Attacking The Fortress 106
On the Recovery of the Patient, Etc. 108
On the Curse of Deities 112
Master-Servant Relations 115
Future With Another Master............................... 117
Recovery of Lost Property 119
Identity of Thief 134
On Meals 141
On Dreams... 148
On Special Questions 149
On Sport... 150
On Disputes... 151
On The Traveller... 153
Release of the Imprisoned Traveller.................. 154

Queries Bearing on Ships, etc.	158
Truth of Rumours	160
On Purchase And Sale	161
On Crops	163

Chapter 4: Miscellaneous Matters ... 165

General Judgment of Houses	167
On The Time Factor	169
First Process	171
Second Process	171
Third Process	171
One's Own Thinking	174
On Sexual Matters	181
On Trade And Commerce	183
Individual's Future	185
On Tajaka Aspects	186
Ithasala Yoga	188
Easarapha Yoga	190
Naktha Yoga	190
Yamaya Yoga	192
Kamboola Yoga	192

Some Examples ... 195

I. Any Likelihood of Becoming Rich?	196
II. Mother's Longevity	197
III. Getting A Child	199
IV. Is the Absent Person Alive or Dead?	200

V. Illness 202
VI. Marriage 203
VII. End of a Strike 205
VIII. Recovery Of Stolen Property 206
IX. Outcome of a Law Suit 208
X. Foreign Travel 209
XI. Leaving the Present Job 210
XII. Profession 212

Index of Technical Terms 214

Preface

I am glad to note Messrs Motilal Banarasidaas International is bringing out a fresh edition of the long awaited classical work Prasna Tantra said to be written by Neelakanta. This text is one of the best books on horary astrology which deals with the subject in great detail. Prasna is one of the branches of Hora, the predictive part of Jyotisha. The text gives simple methods to answer questions on almost all aspects of life and situations one comes across in day to day life also.

The translation by my revered father Dr. B.V. Raman, *Father of Modern Astrology*, is lucid and simple so that even a beginner has no difficulty in navigating through the Prasna world. A careful study of this translation enables one to predict answers to specific questions that trouble the querent relating to different aspects of life like lost articles, missing persons, marital matters, legal issues, job interviews, decisions on investing, missing dogs and other pets, medical conditions, surgery and such other matters that confront most people in their lives.

I thank Mr. J.P. Jain and Mr. Abhishek Jain of Motilal Banarasidaas International, who have been with us in our mission of Jyotisha publishing Dr. B.V. Raman's works since decades, for making available this compact but comprehensive text and its translation to all enthusiasts of Jyotisha.

Date: October 3, 2025   **Gayatri Devi Vasudev**

General Introduction

Horary astrology is the most important branch of the three divisions of the astrological science, the other two being *Jataka* (predictive astrology) and *Muhurtha* (electional astrology). It takes as the basis for predicting future events, the horoscope set for the moment a query is put. Horary has a further advantage over the judicial in the sense that the time of query is known accurately. In fact the time at which a query is put is the time of birth of the intention or desire in the mind of the querent and hence of great significance. The question must be seriously put if the answer is earnestly desired and if correct results are to be obtained. Any questions posed light-heartedly or with mischievous intention should be dismissed by the astrologer. Horary astrology is the art of perceiving the relation between the thought as it arises in the mind and the pattern of the heavens at the moment. This gives a clue for forecasting an event. Hence horary astrology is the most practical and useful branch of knowledge.

Prasna Tantra, an English translation of which is herewith presented, is a treatise on horary astrology, written by Neelakanta Daivagnya. According to some authorities, it is not an independent treatise, but a part of Neelakanta's larger work *Tajaka Neelakanteeya*, being the 3rd or last *Tantra* or division, the other two being *Samgnatantra* (preliminaries) and *Varshatantra* (the annual horoscope). Whether an independent treatise or a part of a larger work, it has its own uniqueness as dealing clearly and in simple language with important aspects of horary astrology.

There are any number of treatises on this branch of astrology written by ancient masters, such as *Chappanna* or *Shat panchasika, Lampaka, Prasnagnana, Prasnabhushana, Prasnasindhu, Prasna Chintamani, Bhuvana Deepika, Jinendramala, Krishneeya* and *Prasna Marga*, the last being the most comprehensive and elaborate exposition of Horary. *Prasna Marga* has been translated by me into English with elaborate notes and it is expected to be out by the end of 1979.

My choice of *Prasna Tantra* for translation into English was due to three reasons. First, it is compact, yet comprehensive. Second, the treatise is clear and the principles given in its pages are in a large measure applicable to modern conditions. And third, in my practice most of the predictions made by me essentially based on this book have been remarkably fulfilled.

The author of this book is said to be Neelakanta Daivagnya. From his own Tajaka and from other collateral sources, it has been gathered that he came from a family of astrologers. He was the grandson of Chinthamani Daivagnya, son of Anantha Daivagnya and brother of Rama Daivagnya and belonged to the Gothra of Gargya. In the last part of his *Varshatantra*, Neelakanta records that he composed this book on the eighth day of the bright half of Aswija of Saka Year 1509 which means 1567 A.D. There is also evidence that he hailed from Vidarbha and that he was about 43 or 44 years old when he wrote this book. While the first two parts (of his larger work), viz., *Samgnatantra* and *Varshatantra* have the commentaries of one Viswanatha Daivagnya, probably written in Saka 1551 (A.D. 1639), no commentaries have been written on the last division which may be said to constitute the independent volume of *Prasna Tantra*. In translating the original into English, the main object has been to bring the spirit of the author rather than the letter

Astrology is a technical subject and in attempting to convey ideas from a highly suggestive and perfect language like Sanskrit into a modern and developing language like English certain confusion of sense cannot be entirely ruled out. It is not a literal translation I have given. But it is a liberal rendering, the object being to make accessible to the Indian public who have a limited knowledge in Sanskrit and also to the Western world where, in recent times, interest in the study of Hindu astrology has been growing by leaps and bounds, a system of Horary astrology in which they will find sufficient information of practical utility. It is for the learned readers to judge how far I have been successful in my humble endeavours.

Prasna Tantra has been divided into four chapters, *viz.*, Prasna Vichara (preliminaries), Bhava Prasna (questions bearing on different houses), Visesha Prasna (special questions) and Prakirnakadhyaya (concluding remarks).

The first chapter deals with such details as the utility of Prasna, planetary characteristics and avasthas, planetary natures, and matters to be inquired into from different houses.

The second chapter is quite comprehensive. It gives combinations for judging the outcome of questions bearing on different houses.

The third chapter deals with specific questions such as the return of a man gone away from home; whether he is alive or dead; whether or not he will return; illness; whether the patient will recover, nature of illness; diagnosis, etc.; leaving employment and seeking another job; disputes, litigation, etc.; success and failure; theft and loss of articles, the age, sex, etc., of the thief, whether the article is lost completely or recoverable and if latter how it could be recovered; children; marriage; dreams, food, hunting, quarrels, incarceration, about ships on sea, purchase and sale, planting of crops, etc. The fourth chapter covers questions such as: gain of money, general outlook, time of gain, thought-reading, enquiry about women, nature of intimacy with women, nature of weather and crops, etc. The chapter is concluded with some important information on aspects and yogas considered in Tajaka Astrology.

The treatment throughout has been comprehensive. Sometimes there is also a certain jumbling of subjects dealt with. For instance, while in Chapter II questions bearing on marriage and children are treated, the same subjects are again repeated in Chapter III in greater detail. On the whole, the entire gamut of horary astrology has been covered skilfully leaving to the discretion of the astrologer, how best he could adapt the principles to answer questions even not covered in the book.

General Introduction

The aspects considered in this book are those of the Tajaka system. The principle aspects, to put in simple language, are the sextile (60°), square (90°), opposition (180°), trine (120°) and conjunction (0°). An aspect by itself has no orb. But, planets have orbs of operation (deepthamsas). They are the Sun 15°, the Moon 12°, Mars 7°, Mercury 7°, Jupiter 9°, Venus 7° and Saturn 9°. No mundane aspects are considered. Though the nature of an aspect and conjunction may be said to depend upon the nature of the planets in aspect, the square and opposition are generally held to be inauspicious while the trine and sextile are held to give rise to auspicious results. Conjunctions are favourable with benefic planets and evil with malefic planets. For instance, a conjunction of Saturn and Mars is definitely evil and threatens serious consequences. A conjunction of Jupiter and Venus is equally good and denotes auspiciousness.

In horary astrology, planets become distinguished as significators. For instance, the lord of the 3rd is the significator of brothers. If he happens to be, say Saturn, and the ascendant lord is Jupiter and if they are in conjunction, the brother (signified by Jupiter) would be adversely affected if the question relates to mutual relations of the two brothers.

Yogas in Tajaka system arise on the basis of applying exact and separating aspects. For further details I would refer my readers to my book *Varshaphal* or *The Hindu Progressed Horoscope*. It deals fully with the Tajaka system.

As regards the significations of planets, Neelakanta has no doubt dealt with them in a fairly exhaustive manner. But we can also have recourse to the significations suggested in other authoritative classics such as *Prasna Marga* and *Krishneeya*.

In interpretation of horary charts certain niceties have to be observed. The lord of the ascendant is always the significator of the querent or his agent though the ascendant and the planets in the ascendant are also important as co-significators. The significator of the event is the ruler of the house concerned. For example the significator of marriage is the lord of the 7th though planets occupying the 7th will also have a role of their own to play. Matters pertaining to health can be studied from the 1st house but illness is indicated by the 6th house. Money matters come under the 2nd but lands and immovable property are signified by the 4th house. Further details about events signified by different houses can be found in the body of the text.

If a querent puts a question, say pertaining to his brother's wife, then we have to consult the 9th house as it is the 7th from the 3rd house. Similarly, a stolen article belonging to a friend has reference to the 4th from 11th (friend). *i.e.*, 2nd house. The closer the Yoga (Ithasala, etc.), the more certain will be the result. If in a question bearing on marriage, the aspect between the rulers of ascendant and the 7th is a square, the event will no doubt happen but certain obstacles will have to be overcome. The Moon's situation always gives a clue to the mind of the querent or his agent. In order to determine a correct answer, the different shades of evidence have to be carefully weighed and assessed.

The astrologer must get into the root of the question and boldly declare the answer avoiding subjective factors. All questions should always be related to their appropriate houses and the planets located therein or connected with the houses by ownership, etc., should be carefully considered.

Translation of light is another factor considered in this book. When a planet separates from one that is slower than itself and overtakes another by conjunction or aspect, there is translation of light. The object of a query will be realised through the help of a person signified by the translating planet. Thus if in a question bearing on marriage, Mercury translates the light of the lord of the 7th to the lord of the 1st, the result will turn out favourably through the person indicated by the translating planet if the aspect is good. If the aspect is evil, then there will be failure or disappointment through the person signified by the translating planet.

As in horoscopy, very often the time-factor is a hard nut to crack in horary astrology too. The most important part of a question is when the expected result or event will occur. There are no doubt rules given in texts on horary astrology but most of them are not found to be quite reliable. It occurs to me that every case must be decided on the nature of the question concerned. Suppose a question relating to birth of an issue is put when the woman is in an advanced stage of pregnancy and at the time of the query, the lords of the ascendant and the significator are 2° apart from each other. Then we can safely say that the delivery will take place within two weeks and the probable date can be fixed on the basis of transits. If a similar distance (conjunction or favourable aspect) is found between the significators, say in respect of a question on marriage, decide the time on the basis of the movable, fixed or common nature of the sign the significator is in. According to the famous work *Krishneeya*, the number of constellations intervening between the ascendant and the constellation occupied by the significator indicates the number of days, provided the ascendant is in a fixed sign. This is to be doubled or trebled according as the Lagna is a common or movable sign respectively.

Another method given by the same work is as follows: Multiply the number of signs intervening between the ascendant and the sign held by the significator by 12. The product represents the number of days, months or years according as the ascendant is a movable, a common or a fixed sign. Both the above two methods have not been found quite satisfactory.

A more satisfactory method is to consider the number of degrees between the aspect of the ascendant lord and the significator as representing the number of days, weeks, or months according as the ascendant is movable, common or fixed.

The other method which could be used with considerable success is to consider the question chart, as Varshaphal chart, calculate the Varshaphal Dasas and then time the result. This method has a drawback because, the timing is to be confined to within 12 months. The reader will do well to adopt the method appealing to him in the light of the practical examples given in this book. It is generally difficult to judge the time of occurrence with accuracy. But by practice a student of astrology can instinctively feel which method he should adopt and he can generally be successful.

Horary astrology is a system of prognostication which demonstrates that in the time at which a query is put lies imbedded seeds of the result. The astrologer in his interpretation of the horary chart should be assisted by promptings from the great Divine.

The astrologer who practises this branch of astrology has certain moral responsibilities. If for instance, a query is put about the death of an ailing father, the answer should not be readily given. The astrologer should first of all find out from the chart, the motive of the querent-whether the question is prompted by love and affection or by sinister motives, such as grabbing the father's property. Similarly questions bearing on the character of the wife or husband should not be answered if the motives of the querents are suspect. Thus the astrological student has certain moral responsibilities towards the society and his art should not be used for harming others or for creating fear, panic or suffering.

A novice in Horary astrology must be very careful in interpreting the Prasna chart.

With my humble capacity I have tried my level best to present an English translation of Prasna Tantra as lucidly as possible and it is for the educated public to judge how far I have been successful in this endeavour. While placing this translation in the hands of my readers I crave their indulgence for any fault that may have crept in.

If the book should prove instructive and useful to my readers, I shall feel myself rewarded.

Bangalore   **B. V. RAMAN**
08-08-1969

। श्रीरस्तु ॥

।: प्रश्नतन्त्र : ॥

Chapter 1

Uses of Horary Astrology

दैवज्ञस्य हि दैवेन सदसत्फलवाञ्छया ।
अवश्यं गोचरे मर्त्यः सर्वः समुपनीयते ॥ १ ॥

अश्रौषीच्च पुरा विष्णोर्ज्ञानार्थे समुपस्थितः ।
वचनं लोकनाथोऽपि ब्रह्मा प्रश्नादिनिर्णयम् ॥ २ ॥

Stanzas 1 and 2: According to the opinion of astrologers, all those human beings who will be impelled (by Daiva) wish to know the current good and bad nature of things in their lives.

Once upon a time, even the Lord of the world Brahma approached Vishnu to learn horary astrology.

NOTES

The importance of horary astrology is stressed in the first two stanzas. Every one that is impelled by Daiva or an inner urge will become inclined to approach an astrologer to know about his immediate future. Here 'Daiva' is the unknown factor and usually means one's past Karma. As a result of one's past Karma, one gets *prerana* or inspiration or the urge to consult an astrologer and horary astrology reveals the future on the basis of the current dispositions of planets.

How to Put A Query?

तस्मान्नृपः कुसुमरत्नफलाग्रहस्तः प्रातः प्रणम्य वरयेदपि
प्राङ्मुखस्थः ।
होराङ्गशास्त्रकुशलान् हितकारिणश्च संहृत्य दैवगणकान्
सकृदेव पृच्छेत् ॥ ३ ॥

Stanza 3: One should approach a learned astrologer of pleasant disposition, early in the morning, with fruits, flowers and money and facing the east and after making due obeisance to the astrologer, put only one question of an auspicious nature.

NOTES

According to tradition the querist, be he a commoner or a prince, should follow a certain procedure before putting questions to an astrologer. Early morning is considered to be suitable for consultation.. Flowers, fruits, etc., indicate auspiciousness. An astrologer is a *daivagnya* or decipherer of the intention of God. Therefore he is to be approached with a certain reverence and humility. It is only an astrologer of a "pleasant disposition" that deserves to be consulted. The above three stanzas are attributed to Varahamihira.

The True Astrologer

दशभेदं ग्रहगणितं जातकमवलोक्य निस्वशेषमपि ।
यः कथयति शुभमशुभं तस्य न मिथ्या भवेद्वाणी ॥ ४ ॥

Stanza 4: The predictions of one well-versed in the ten kinds of calculating planetary longitudes and proficient in astrological lore cannot go wrong.

NOTES

There is no need to explain the different astronomical methods of calculating planetary dispositions as today, the castings are invariably done according to Panchangas or modern ephemerides. The above sloka is attributed to Utpala, the commentator of *Brihat Jataka*. Hence the reference here to the word 'Jataka' is taken by some as proficiency in *Brihat Jataka*.

समरसारे—विनयावनताय दीयमाना ।
प्रभवेत्कल्पलतेव सत्फलायेति ॥ ५ ॥

Stanza 5: In the hands of men of learning culture and humility successful results alone are possible.

NOTES

The *Jatakarnava* says: "According to God Siva's own words, predictions should not be given to persons who are mean, arrogant, atheistic, violent and devoid of decent behaviour."

About the Querist

ऋजुरयमनृजुवाऽयं प्रष्टा पूर्वं परीक्ष्य लग्नबलात् ।
गणकेन फलं वाच्यं दैवं तच्चित्तगं स्फुरति ॥ १ ॥

Stanza 1: Whether the person is sincere or not in putting the question should first be ascertained on the strength of the ascendant. The astrologer should then study the good and bad aspects of the query and his prediction will be duly inspired.

लग्नस्थे शशिनि, शनौ केन्द्रस्थे ज्ञे दिनेशरश्मिगते ।
भौमज्ञयाः समदृशा लग्नगचंद्रेऽनृजुः प्रष्टा ॥ २ ॥

लग्ने शुभग्रहयुते सरल: क्रूरान्विते भवेत्कुटिल: ।
लग्नेऽस्ते सौम्यदृशा विधुगुरुदृष्ट्या च सरलोऽयम् ॥ ३ ॥

यदि गुरुबुधयोरेक: पश्यत्यस्ताधिपञ्च रिपुदृष्ट्या ।
तत्कुटिल: प्रष्टा खल्वनयोरेकस्तयो: साधु: ॥४॥

Stanzas 2 to 4: The querist's intention will not be honest if (a) the Moon is in the ascendant, Saturn is in a quadrant and Mercury is combust; (b) Mars and Mercury aspect the Moon in the ascendant; (c) a malefic joins the ascendant; (d) Jupiter or Mercury cast an inimical glance on the lord of the 7th. His intention will be sincere if (a) a benefic plant joins the ascendant; (b) if Mars or full Moon and Jupiter aspect the ascendant; and (c) Jupiter or Mercury throws a friendly aspect on the lord of the seventh.

NOTES

The combinations are simple and do not require an explanation. Astrological practitioners must be well aware of the fact that some persons put questions either for fun or for testing the astrologer and therefore have dishonest intentions. If the astrologer feels by a study of the chart that the queriest is not sincere, he should decline to give any prediction. No test questions should be entertained.

Mercury (according to Tajaka) becomes combust 'if within 14 degrees' from the Sun. The inimical and friendly aspects referred to in stanza 4 are the square and trine respectively. If Jupite squares lord of the 7th, it is an inimical aspect.

Answering More Than One Query

आदिमं लग्नतो ज्ञानं चन्द्रस्थानाद्द्वितीयकम् ।
सूर्यस्थानात्तृतीयं स्यात्तुर्यं जीवगृहाद्भवेत् ॥
बुधभृर्ग्वोर्बली यः स्वात्तद्गृहात्पञ्चमं पुनः ॥ ५ ॥

सम्यग्विचार्य लग्नं ब्रूयात्प्रश्नं सकृद्यथाशास्त्रम् ।
यस्त्वेकं ब्रूतेऽसौ तस्य न मिथ्या भवेद्वाणी ॥ ६ ॥

Stanzas 5 and 6: The first query is to be read from the ascendant, the second from the Moon, the third from the Sun, the fourth from Jupiter and the fifth from the stronger of the planets Mercury or Venus.

It is the dictum of the astrological science that a query has to be answered by a proper assessment of the ascendant. If only one question is answered, the prediction cannot go wrong.

NOTES

The considered opinion of the author appears to be that at a time only one question has to be tackled if the prediction is to be correct. When a series of questions are put at a particular moment, they have to be answered thus:

1st question—Ascendant;

2nd question—Sign occupied by the Moon;

3rd question—Sign occupied by the Sun;

4th question—Sign occupied by Jupiter;

5th question — Sign occupied by Mercury or Venus.

In regard to the 5th question, the Rasi held by either Mercury or Venus whichever is stronger should be considered.

In support of his view that only one query should be answered from a horary chart, Nilakanta quotes from *Prasna Chinthamani* according to which after making all the calculations only one query should be answered.

Planetary Avasthas

दीप्ताद्यं दशभेदं च ग्रहाणां भांशजं फलं ।
विचार्य प्रवदेद्यस्तु तस्योक्तं नान्यथा भवेत् ॥ ७ ॥

Stanza 7: One should predict by examining the ten planetary states such as Deeptha, etc., and such a prediction will not go wrong.

NOTES

The ten avasthas are: (1) deeptha—exaltation, (2) deena—debilitation, (3) muditha—friendly sign, (4) swastha—own house, (5) suptha—inimical house, (6) nipeeditha—vanquished, (7) mushita—combust, (8) pariheena—descending towards debility, (9) suveerya—ascending towards exaltation, and (10) athiveerya—excess of benefic vargas.

Results of Avasthas

दीप्ते सिद्धिश्व कार्याणां दीने दुःख समागमः ।
स्वस्थे कीर्तिस्तथा लक्ष्मीरानन्द्रो मुदिते महान् ॥ ८ ॥

सुप्ते रिपुभयं दुःखं धनहानिर्निपीडिते ।
सुपीते परिहीने व कार्यनाशोऽर्थसंक्षयः ॥ ९ ॥

गजाश्वकनकावाप्तिः सुदीर्ये रत्नसंपदः ।
अधिवीर्ये राज्यलब्धिर्ग्रहैमित्रार्थसङ्गमः ॥ १० ॥

Stanzas 8, 9 and 10: In a Prasna chart planets subject to the different avasthas are capable of conferring the following results:

Deeptha—success in the undertaking; deena—sorrow; swastha—fame; muditha—gain of wealth and happiness; suptha—sorrow and fear from enemies; nipeeditha—loss of money; mushita and pariheena—failure and loss of money; suveerya—access to conveyance and gold; and athiveerya—political success and valuable contacts.

NOTES

In the above stanzas, the results of planets subject to different avasthas have been given. In the translation, what is relevant to modern conditions has been retained. For example, a planet in suveerya is said to confer elephants (gaja), horses (aswa) and gold (kanaka). In the translation, the word "conveyance" is submitted as in modern times. It is very rare that elephants and horses are used for locomotion. The planets can give the ascribed results only when they influence the signification concerned. If, for instance, a query pertains to illness and the significator happens to be in *suveeryavastha*, access to gold cannot be read. The interpretation must be consistent with the nature of the question.

Planetary Indications

पूर्वः सत्वं नृपस्तातः क्षवं ग्रीष्मोऽरुणश्चलः ।
मधु वैत्तिकोधातुः शूरः सूक्ष्मकचो रविः ॥ ११ ॥

Stanza 11: The Sun signifies east, satwic nature, royalty, father, Kshatriya caste, heat, blood-red colour, wavering temperament, honey-coloured eyes, phlegm, minerals, courage and thin hair.

कफी वर्षा मृदुर्माता पयो गौरश्व सात्विकः ।
जीवो वश्यश्वरो वृत्तो मारुतांशो विधुः सुदृक् ॥ १२ ॥

Stanza 12: The Moon signifies phlegm, rainy season, softness, mother, milk 'white colour', satwic nature, living, beings, Vaisya caste, swiftness, circular shape, wind, and charming eyes.

ग्रीष्मः क्षत्रतमो रक्तो याम्यः सेनाग्रणीश्वरः ।
युवा धातुश्चः पिङ्गाक्षः क्रूरः पित्तं शिखी कुजः ॥ १३॥

Stanza 13: Mars indicates Greeshma (June-July) season, Kshatriya caste, blood-red, south, commander-in-chief, wavering nature, youthfulness, dhatu (minerals), white (peeta), eyes, cruelty, bilious constitution, sikhi (possessing a tuft).

शरदीशो हरिर्दीर्घः षण्ढो मूलं कुमारकः ।
लिपिज्ञ उत्तरेशश्व शूद्रः सौम्यस्त्रिधातुकः ॥ १४ ॥

Stanza 14: Mercury signifies Sarat season (October-November), bluish hue, tall body, impotency, moola (minerals), heir-apparent, ability in writing, north, Sudra caste, a mixture of windy, phlegmatic and bilious nature.

सत्त्वं वित्तो हिमः श्लेष्मा दीर्घो मन्त्री द्विजो नरः ।
मध्यैशानी कफी जीवो मधुपिंगलधृक् तथा ॥ १५ ॥

Stanza 15: Jupiter rules satwic nature, wealth, cold, phlegmatic constitution, tall body, prime-minister,

Brahmins, male sex, midday, north-east and honey-coloured eyes.

शुक्रः शान्तो द्विजो नारी वश्यो मन्त्री चरः सितः ।
आग्नेयोदिक्कुफश्चाम्लः कुटिलासितमूर्धजः ॥ १६ ॥

Stanza 16: Venus signifies peace, Brahmin, women, subordinates, prime-minister, wavering nature, white colour, south-east, phelgmatic constitution, sour taste, and curly hair.

कृष्णास्तमः कृशो वृद्धः षण्ढो मूलान्त्यजाऽलसः ।
शिशिरः पवनः क्रूरः पश्चिमो वातुलः शनिः ॥ १७ ॥

Stanza 17: Saturn signifies black colour, sinful nature, weakness, old age, impotence, moola (minerals), untouchables, remissness, Sisira season (March-April), wind, cruel nature, west, and windy constitution.

राहुर्धातुः शिखी मूलं शेषमन्यच्च मन्दवत् ।
चिन्तनीयं विलग्ने ज्ञात् केन्द्रगाद्वा बलाधिकात् ॥ १८ ॥

Stanza 18: Rahu signifies 'dhatu', tuft of hair, vegetables (moola) and events indicated by Saturn, becomes strong in a Kendra from Mercury or the ascendant.

NOTES

The Karakatwas of planets listed here are fairly exhaustive. They will be highly useful in answering a variety of questions bearing on theft, profession, persons who have run away, sickness, etc. It is also worth taking into account the significations assigned to planets in other classical astrological works.

In addition to the Karakatwas given above which are fairly exhaustive, the following significations may also be noted. *The Sun*—palaces, aristocracy, goldsmiths, medicines, diseases of the heart and eye, pride, independent spirit, humanity and patrimony; *the Moon*—agriculture, pearls, women, eyes, royalty, sailors, aquatic plants, female diseases, gout, psychosis and abscess; *Mars*—fire, incendiarism, sex-urge, fighting spirit, hazards, boasting, quarrels, criminal acts, sedition, rashness, thieving, violence, courage, surgeons and physicians, barbers, chemists, army, high fevers, cuts and wounds, injuries, bloody complaints, surgical operations, ulcers carbuncles, fistula, piles and the stone in the kidney, bladder, etc.; *Mercury*—writing, mathematics, poets, architecture, impotency, wit and humour, accountants and actuaries, merchants, trade eloquence, tale-bearer, scandals, communications, neurosis, idiocy, newspapers, ambassadors, clerks, astrologers, rheumatism, nervous troubles, brain disease, memory defects and dumbness; *Jupiter*—Brahmins, Vedic scholars, priests, children, charity, reverence, sobriety, judges, ministers, religious heads and institution, liver troubles, diabetes, palpitation and flatulence; *Venus*—brightness, good manners, artistes, music, dancing, love, fashion, cleanliness, affection, virtue and vice, bed-pleasures, hotels, liquor, musicians, embroiders, wife, perfumes, cow-herds and beauty-shops, venereal complaints and diseases arising from easy living and lust, generative organs and hernia; *Saturn*—manual labour, brick-laying, masonry, restraint, reserved nature, hair, begging, miners, tinners, factory-workers, shepherds, wasting disease, jaundice, haemorrhoids, water-closets, latrines, sinks and dirty-linen; *Rahu and Ketu* resemble Saturn and Mars.

Events to Know from Different Houses

सौख्यमायुर्वयो जातिरारोग्यं लक्षण गुणम् ।
क्लेशाकृती रुपवर्णास्तनोश्चिन्त्या विचक्षणैः ॥ १९ ॥

Stanza 19: From the first house is to be discovered one's happiness, longevity, age, caste, health, disposition, nature, sorrow, appearance and complexion.

मुक्ताफलन्च माणिक्यम् रत्नधातुधनाम्बरम् ।
हयकार्याध्व विज्ञानं वित्तस्थानद्विलोकयेत् ॥ २० ॥

Stanza 20: The second house rules pearls, precious stones and minerals and wealth, apparel, work pertaining to horses and roads.

भगिनीभ्रातृभृत्यानां दासकर्मकृतामपि ।
कुर्वीत वीक्षणं विद्वान् सम्यग्दृश्चिक्यवेश्मतः ॥ २१ ॥

Stanza 21: The third house rules sisters, brothers, servants and those that perform menial work.

वाटीकाखलकक्षेत्र महौषधिनिधीनपि ।
विवरादिप्रवेशं च पश्योत्पातालतो बुधः ॥ २२ ॥

Stanza 22: The fourth rules tracts of land, places where plants are thrashed, tracts abounding in vegetation, special medicines, treasure troves and crevices.

गर्भापत्यविनेयानां मन्वसंधानयोरपि ।
विद्याबुद्धिप्रबन्धानां सुतस्थाने विनिर्णयः ॥ २३ ॥

Stanza 23: The fifth house has rulership over pregnancy, issues, wanderings, spells and incantations, arbitration, learning, intelligence, and , discourses.

चौरभी रिपुसंग्रामखरोष्ट्रक्रूरकर्मणाम् ।
मातुलाकभृत्यानां रिपुस्थानाद्विनिर्णयः ॥ २४॥

Stanza 24: The sixth house denotes fear from thieves, enemies, fighting, donkeys, diabolical deeds, maternal uncle, fear and obstruction, and servants.

वाणिज्यं व्यवहारं च विवादं च समं परः ।
गमागमकलत्राणि पश्येत्प्राज्ञः कलत्रतः ॥ २५ ॥

Stanza 25: From the seventh house should be read trade, transactions, disputes, journeys and wife or husband.

नद्युत्तारेध्ववैषम्ये दुर्गे शात्रवसंकटे ।
नष्टे दुष्टे रणे व्याधौ छिद्रे छिद्रं निरीक्षयेत् ॥ २६ ॥

Stanza 26: The eighth house rules river crossing, wayside suffering, hills, trouble from enemies, lost property, evil deeds, battles, diseases and clandestine deeds.

वापीकूपतडागादिप्रपादेवगृहाणि च ।
दीक्षां यात्रां मठं धर्म धर्मानिश्चिन्त्य कीर्तयेत् ॥ २७ ॥

Stanza 27: The ninth house signifies tanks, wells, lakes, water-reservoirs, deities, places of worship, maths, vows (penance), pilgrimage and righteousness.

राज्यं मुद्रां परं पुण्यं स्थानं तातं प्रयोजनम् ।
वृष्ट्यादिव्योमवृत्तांतं व्योमस्थानान्निरीक्षयेत् ॥ २८॥

Stanza 28: Events to be ascertained from the tenth house are Government, authority, meritorious deeds. virtue, position, father, essential things, rainfall and celestial phenomena.

गजाश्वयानवस्त्राणि सस्यकाञ्चनकन्यकाः ।
विद्वान् विद्यार्थयोलोभं लक्षयेल्लाभलग्नतः ॥ २९॥

Stanza 29: The eleventh house signifies elephant and horse-rides, clothes, the staple food, gold, daughter and gain of wealth.

त्यागभोगविवादेषु दानेष्टकृषिकर्मसु ।
व्यवस्थानेषु सर्वेषु विद्धि विद्वद् व्ययं व्ययात् ॥३०॥

Stanza 30: The 12th house rules renunciation, enjoyment, disputes, charity, cultivation and institutional expenditure.

NOTES

The significations given to the planets as above do not differ much from the significations suggested in books on Parasari Astrology. The 9th house is said to rule father but as per stanza 28, the tenth signifies father. A more elaborate description of significations is to be found in Satyacharya's *Dhruvanadi* and the reader will do well to read it. Whether the significations mentioned by Satyacharya can be made use of in Horary Astrology is a point which can be decided only on the basis of one's experience.

Chapter 2
Bhava Prasna

General Estimate

यो यो भावः स्वामिदृष्टे युतो वा सौम्यैर्वा स्यात्तस्यतस्यास्ति वृद्धिः ।
पापैरेवं तस्य भावस्य हानिर्निर्देष्टव्या पृच्छतो जन्मतो वा ॥ १ ॥

Stanza 1: Whether according to horoscopy or horary astrology, whichever Bhavas are associated with or aspected by either their respective lords or benefic planets would gain vitality. The effects will be destroyed if malefics aspect or join them.

NOTES

This is a general principle enumerated in all astrological works. Stanza 1 makes clear the following three combinations:

(i) The Bhava aspected by or associated with its lord will prosper.

(ii) The Bhava aspected by or associated with a benefic planet will also prosper.

(iii) The Bhava aspected by or conjoined with a malefic will lose vitality.

Here by malefics and benefics are meant natural malefics and benefics. A natural malefic ceases to be a malefic the moment he becomes lord of the ascendant.

सौम्ये विलग्ने यदि वा स्ववर्गे शीर्षोदये सिद्धिमुपैति कार्यम् ।
अतो विपर्यस्तमसिद्धिहेतुः कृच्छूरेण संसिद्धिकरं विमिश्रम् ॥ २ ॥

Stanza 2: The object of the question will be fulfilled if benefics join the ascendant or its own vargas rise in the ascendant or the ascendant happens to be a *sirshodaya* sign. If otherwise, the object will not be fulfilled. If the influences are mixed, there will be success after initial setbacks.

NOTES

The above two stanzas are from *Shatpanchasika*.

The object of the querist will be realised when one of the following combinations is present:

(i) The ascendant is joined by benefic planets.

(ii) The ascendant point has own or friendly vargas. (iii) The ascendant happens to be a Sirshodaya sign.

Failure is shown when malefics rise in the ascendant and the ascendant point falls in the vargas of malefic planets. When the benefic and malefic influences are balanced, there will be ultimate success after initial reverses.

The *Sirshodaya Rasis* (signs rising by head) are Gemini, Leo, Virgo. Libra, Scorpio and Aquarius. The rest are *Prushtodaya Rasis* or signs rising by their hinder parts.

Success of Object in View

लग्नपतिर्यदि लग्नं कार्याधिपतिश्व वीक्षते कार्यम् ।
लग्नाधीशः कार्यं कार्येशः पश्यति विलग्नम् ॥ ३ ॥

लग्नेशः कार्येशं विलोकयेल्लग्नपम् तु कार्येशः ।
शीतगुहृष्टो सत्यां परिपूर्णं कार्यसंसिद्धिः ॥ ४ ॥

Stanza 3 and 4: The ascendant lord aspects the ascendant the and the significator aspects (appropriate) house; or the ascendant lord aspects the house and the significator aspects ascendant; or the ascendant lord and the significator are in mutual aspect; or the Moon aspects both the significator and the ascendant lord the object of the query will be completely fulfilled.

NOTES

If the significator is the lord of the house a particular query pertains to (Karyapa or Karyesa). Thus if a query relates to acquisition of wealth, the significator will be the lord of the 2nd; if it pertains to marriage the significator will be the lord of the 7th. As the stanzas are quite simple to understand, further explanation does not seem to be necessary. The above two stanzas are from *Bhuyana Pradeepa.*

कथयन्ति पादयोगं पश्यति सौम्यो न लग्नपो लग्नम् ।
लग्नाधिपं च पश्यति शुभग्रहश्रार्धयोगोऽत्र ॥ ५ ॥

एकः शुभो ग्रहो यदि पश्यति लग्नाधिपं विलग्नं वा ।
पादो न योगमाहुस्तदा बुधाः कार्य संसिद्धौ ॥ ६ ॥

लग्नपतौ दशमे सति शुभग्रहौ द्वौ त्रयोऽथवा लग्नम् ।
पश्यन्ति यदि तदानीमाहुर्योगं विभागोनम् ॥ ७ ॥

लग्नेश दर्शने सति पश्यन्तः पूर्णयोगकराः ।
क्रूरावेक्षणवर्ण्यश्चन्द्रः सौम्याश्च खेचरा लग्नम् ॥ ८ ॥

Stanzas 5 to 8: The chances of success will be one-fourth, half, three-fourths or full according as (a) the ascendant is not aspected either by its lord or a benefic; (b) the ascendant lord is aspected by benefics; (c) even one benefic aspects the ascendant or its lord; or the ascendant lord or 2 or 3 benefics are in the 10th; or three benefics aspect the ascendant; and (d) the ascendant is aspected by its lord, or the Moon is free from affliction and benefics aspect the Lagna.

NOTES

The above four stanzas give combinations indicative of different degrees of *Karyasiddhi* (success) attending. a query. They may be detailed thus :-

(a) (i) The rising sign is devoid of the lord's aspect— 25% success.

    (ii) The rising sign is devoid of the aspect of a benefic — 25% success.

(b) Benefics aspect lord of the ascendant — 50%

(c) (i) At least one benefic aspects the ascendant or its lord

    (ii) The lord of the rising sign or 2 or 3 benefics are in the 10th   } 75%

    (iii) three benefics aspect ascendant

(d) (i) Ascendant is aspected by its lord

    (ii) The Moon is unafflicted and the Ascendant is aspected by benefics   } 100%

Malefic Combinations

क्रूराक्रान्तः क्रूरयुतः क्रूरदृष्टश्च यो ग्रहः ।
विरश्मिताँ प्रपन्नश्च सोऽनिष्टफलदायकः ॥ ९ ॥

Stanza 9: Such planets defeated in war by malefics, those associated with or aspected by malefics and planets in combustion give unfavourable results.

NOTES

Two planets are said to be in war when they are in exact conjunction. Planets become combust when they are situated within certain distances from the Sun thus on either side: Mars 12°, Mercury 8°, Jupiter 9°, Venus 7°, and Saturn 9°.

अमुकं गदेति कार्यं कदा भविष्यत्यमुत्र पृच्छायाम् ।
लग्नाधिपतिः कार्ये लग्नं कार्याधिपः पश्येत् ॥ १० ॥

लग्नस्थः कार्येशः पश्यति चेल्लग्नपं तदैव भवेत् ।
तत्कार्यं यद्यन्यस्थितं तदा सत्वरं न स्यात् ॥ ११ ॥

पश्यति तदा च लग्नं द्रक्ष्यति चन्द्रं विलग्नपं च यदा
लग्ने कार्ये च यदा द्वयोश्च योगे तदा सिद्धिः ॥ १२ ॥

Stanzas 10 to 12: A query such as "when will I succeed" should be answered thus: There will be success when (a) the lord of the ascendant aspects the signification and the significator aspects the ascendant; or (b) the significator being situated in the ascendant aspects the lord of the ascendant; (c) or the significator occupying a sign other than the ascendant aspects the lord of the ascendant; or (d) the significator aspect the Lagna, Lagna lord or the Moon; (e) or the ascendant lord and the significator are mutually connected either in the ascendant or in the Bhava (house) concerned. In (b) and (c) the success will be immediate or delayed respectively.

NOTES

Stanzas 10 to 12 are important. They enable one to answer, whether the object of the query will be realised immediately or after some delay. The terms signification and significator used by us in the translation mean the Bhava or house in question and its lord respectively. Thus in a query "when will one succeed in getting married", the signification has reference to the 7th house and the significator, to the lord of the 7th. There will be marriage very soon if (a) the 7th lord occupying the ascendant aspects the lord of the rising sign; (b) or the marriage takes place after delay if the 7th lord not occupying the Lagna aspects the ascendant lord.

यदि लग्नपं न पश्यति कार्याधीशो विलग्नमथ तस्य ।
कार्यस्य हानिरुक्ता लग्नमृते किमपि नो वाच्यम् ॥ १३ ॥

Stanza 13: The object of the query will not be fulfilled if the significator does not aspect the ascendant or its lord. In a query pertaining to "success or failure" no house other than the ascendant can be considered important.

NOTES

In the following verses culled from other Tajaka sources such as *Prasna Deepika*, etc., Neelakanta deals with queries bearing on the twelve houses.

First House

भूतं भवद्भविष्यन्मम किं कथयेति जातपृच्छायाम् ।
लग्नपतेः शशिनो वा बलमन्वेष्यं बलाभावे ॥ १ ॥

Stanza 1: If a person puts the question 'how about my past, present and future', first ascertain the strengths of the ascendant and the Moon. If both are weak, the object of the query will fail.

दृष्ट्वा नवांशकबलं शुभदृग्योगं च सर्वकालेषु ।
प्रष्टुः शुभमादेश्यं विपरीतं व्यत्ययादेषा ॥ २ ॥

Stanza 2: Always note the strength of the Navamsa Lagna. If it is subject to benefic aspects, the querist derives favourable results. Malefic aspects cause unfavourable results.

लग्नेशो मूसरिफो यस्मादतीतमाख्येयम् ।
येन युतस्तस्माद्भवदेश्यं यो योक्ष्यते तस्मात् ॥ ३ ॥

Stanza 3: Read the past, present and the future from the planets who are respectively in Musaripha, in conjunction with and in Ithasala with the ascendant lord.

यदि लग्ने लग्नपतिः सौम्ययुतो वा विलोकितः सौम्यैः ।
तत्प्रष्टुर्व्याकुलता शरीरदोषा विनश्यन्ति ॥ ४ ॥

Stanza 4: If the lord of the ascendant is in the ascendant or in conjunction with benefics, the querist will become free from worry and ill-health.

पापो यदि लग्नपतिस्तदा कलिश्चाधिधननाशः ।
सौम्ये निर्वृतिबुद्धिर्द्रव्याप्तिः सौख्यमतुलं च ॥ ५ ॥

Stanza 5: According as the lord of Lagna is a malefic or a benefic, there will be quarrels, illness and loss of money; or mental equilibrium, gain of money and happiness.

NOTES

If a planet is in Musaripha with the ascendant lord, the query pertains to the past; if a planet is in conjunction with the ascendant lord, the query is about the present; if a planet has Ithasala with the ascendant lord, then query bears on the future. The nature of the query etc... should be ascertained from the nature of the planet concerned.

The Musarpha, Ithasala and other Tajaka Yogas have been explained in detail in my book *Varshaphal* and the reader will do well to read it.

If the object is to be fulfilled, then the Lagna and the Moon must be strongly disposed.

If the Navamsa Lagna is connected with benefics' favourable results happen. Otherwise, opposite results will occur.

If the Lagna is occupied by benefics or the lord of Lagna is with benefics, the querist's objects will be fulfilled. He will have health and income. If the ascendant or its lord is afflicted, the querist will lack mental peace, become ill and suffer financial loss.

As in horoscopy the Lagna has always a prominent role to play in Prasna or horary astrology too. The first house always signifies the querent or the person who puts the question.

Between the Lagna and the Moon, the more powerful one has to be considered. The ruler of the ascendant in good aspect with any other Bhava or its lord can indeed promote the results of that Bhava,

A distinction is made by some astrological writers whether a question is radical, i.e., has to be read only from the birth chart, or can be dealt with on the basis of the horary chart. In my humble opinion, questions bearing on all aspects of life can be answered by the horary chart.

Saturn 13-24	Rahu 3-7		
Moon 23-4	11-12-1957 at 9.30 a.m. at Bangalore		
Mars 15-7			Jupiter 13-38
	Sun 26-16 Mercury 16-23	Lagna 1 Venus 12-12 Kethu 3-7	

In the example given herein, the lord of the ascendant Venus, a fast-moving planet is, less in longitude (12° 12') than Jupiter (13° 38') having formed Ithasala Yoga. Therefore the query pertains to the future. Though lord of the ascendant is in the ascendant, he is afflicted by association with Kethu. The Moon is also afflicted. Therefore, the immediate future of the querent will not be good as he has to pass through difficulties and mental worry.

The 1st house signifies the querent, his physical appearance. We can read from it the indications of health, vitality and success. A strong disposition of the ascendant and its lord are a *sine qua non* of benefic results in respect of the events signified by the 1st house. If the query relates to health, you can predict that the querent will continue to have good health when the ruler of the ascendant is free from combustion or conjunction with the lord of the 6tb, 8th or 12th house. The stronger the ascendant lord and the Moon the better it is for health. The ascendant should be free from occupation by a malefic. If the ascendant lord is in Musaripha Yoga and is about to enter Ithasala with a malefic the health will give way and the querent may fall ill shortly. If, on the other hand, the ascendant lord is entering shortly Ithasala with a benefic or is entering his sign of exaltation, etc., the querent will recover shortly if he is ill at the time of query.

If the ascendant is occupied by Mars or Saturn and if the lord has Easaripha with lord of the 8th and also a malefic, the life of the querent is threatened. Considerable skill or interpretative ability is needed to draw correct conclusions.

Second House

धनलाभस्य प्रश्ने लग्नेशेनेन्दुनाऽथ धननाथः ।
कुरुते यदित्थशालं शुभयुतिदृष्ट्यां भवेल्लाभः ॥ ६ ॥

क्रूरग्रहैर्धनस्थैर्दूरे लाभोऽन्यदप्यशुभम् ।
क्रूरमुथशिले धनेशे प्रष्टा म्रियतेऽथवा बिलग्नेशे ॥ ७ ॥

धनधनपतीत्थशाले मंदगतिर्यत्र भावानाम् ।
तनुधनसहजादीनां प्रष्टस्तद्द्वारतो लाभः ॥ ८ ॥

Stanzas 6 to 8: In a query about finance, predict gain of money if the lord of the 2nd is in Ithasala with the lord of Lagna or the Moon; or is in conjunction with or aspected by benefics.

If malefics are in the 2nd, the querist gains money from a distant land and also suffers affliction. If the lord of the 2nd has Muthaseela with malefics, the querist may die.

If the ascendant lord has Ithasala with the 2nd or lord of the 2nd, in whichever Bhava the slower-moving planet is situated gain accrues through that Bhava.

NOTES

The combinations given in stanzas 6 and 7 are simple enough to understand. The 8th stanza says that the gain will be from the source indicated by the Bhava where the slower-moving of the two planets— the Lagna lord and the 2nd lord — is situated.

	Jupiter 9		
			Saturn 11
Ascendant 8			

In the above example, mark Ithasala between, Jupiter (ascendant) and Saturn (lord of the 2nd). Saturn the slower-moving planet, is in the 9th indicating gain through the source signified by the 9th house.

लग्नस्थं चन्द्रजं चन्द्रः क्रूरो वा यदि पश्यति ।
धनलाभो भवत्याशु कित्वनर्थोऽपि पृच्छतः ॥ ९ ॥

Stanza 9: If Mercury occupying the ascendant is aspected by the Moon or a malefic, there will be gain of wealth but also untoward happenings.

चन्द्रलग्नधनत्धीशा दृष्टा युक्ताः परस्परम् ।
धनकेन्द्रत्रिकोणस्थाः सद्यो लाभकराः स्मृताः ॥ १० ॥

Stanza 10: When the Moon, lord of the ascendant and the lord of the 2nd house are in conjunction or in mutual aspect occupying the 2nd or a kendra (quadrant) or a thrikona (trine) there will be immediate gain to the querist.

शुभदस्वामिषड्वर्गे लग्ने सौम्ययुतेक्षिते ।
प्रष्टृस्तात्कालिकी लब्धिरलब्धिस्तु विपर्यये ॥ ११ ॥

Stanza 11: If the lord of the ascendant has benefic Shadvargas and the Lagna is aspected by or associated with benefics, the querist secures immediate gains. Otherwise contrary results will happen.

चतुर्थे सप्तमे चन्द्रे खे रवौ लग्नगे शुभे ।
प्रष्टुः सद्योऽर्थलाभः स्याल्लग्ने वा सुरमन्त्रिणि ॥ १२ ॥

Stanza 12: The Moon in the 4th or the 7th, the Sun in the 10th, a benefic in the ascendant, confer immediate gain of money. The same will be the result if Jupiter occupies the ascendant.

NOTES

The above four slokas are from *Prasna Deepika*.

All matters pertaining to wealth, finance and fortune, money lent, profits, come under the 2nd house. Regarding questions bearing on diseases the 2nd house indicates the neck. Good aspect between the lords of the 1st and 2nd or Dhanakaraka Jupiter always indicates gain and prosperity. It is within our experience, that in queries bearing on financial problems, the ascendant lord in the 2nd always denotes quick removal of poverty. Rahu and Saturn in the 2nd are indicators of poverty or complications in financial matters. The financial gain or benefits can come from sources signified by the Bhava-lord in the 2nd house or in association with the second lord. Thus the lord of the 7th in the 2nd may indicate gain through wife lord of the 10th in the 2nd—through one's own occupation

The planet afflicting the 2nd or the 2nd lord indicates the source of financial distress or trouble. One is cautioned that interpretation should always rest on a correct assessment of the lord and the house. A strong malefic well disposed can indicate gain after much effort. If the lords of the 1st, 2nd and the indicator of wealth, *viz.*, Jupiter are in conjunction in a quadrant or 2nd or 1st or 11th house or if they are in mutual Ithasala, financial prosperity will surely occur. If the aspect involving the above lords is a square or opposition, then we can predict gain with much difficulty. There should be no Musaripha Yoga.

	Mars 22-0		Sun 25-52
			Mercury 6-49 (R) Venus 0-41
	10-7-19-60 about 3-20 p.m.		
			Rahu 26-45
Saturn 22-3 Jupiter 4-27		Ascendant 12-0	

Here is a question: "Whether I shall ever become rich"?

Lord of the ascendant Venus in the 10th in conjunction with Mercury lord of the 9th; lord of the 2nd Mars in his own house in the 7th (house of marriage); Jupiter Dhanakaraka in sextile to the ascendant and in trine to Mars; and Mars lord of the 2nd sextiles the Sun. It was predicted that the native would gain by marriage and that his financial status would considerably increase. The time predicted was when Mars by transit conjoined the Sun lord of the 11th. The native secured a handsome dowry with which he started a broker's business which fetched him huge profits.

Third House

सहजपतिर्यदि सहजं पश्यति चेत्तद्द्वयं शुभैर्दृष्टम् ।
तद् भ्रातरो गतरुजः स्वस्थाः क्रूरेक्षणे वामम् ॥ १३ ॥

Stanza 13: When the lord of the third house aspects the 3rd or if the third house and the lord are aspected by benefics, the health of the querist's brothers will be good and they will be happy. If otherwies, contrary results will happen.

NOTES

If the third house is not aspected by its lord or if the third house and the third lord are afflicted by malefics, the querist's brothers will be ill and they will not be happy. Such an answer assumes that the query pertains to the welfare of brothers.

यदि सहजपति: षष्ठे तत्पतिना सुथशिलेऽथ तन्मांद्यम् ।
षष्ठेशे सहजस्थे सहजपतौ क्रूरिते वाऽपि ॥ १४ ॥

Stanza 14: If the lord of the third is in the sixth and is in Muthaseela with the lord of the 6th; or if the lord of the 6th is in the 3rd or the lord of the 3rd is afflicted, the querent's brothers will be in bad health.

सूर्यस्य रश्मिसंस्थे भयावहं प्रष्टुरादेश्यम् ।
षष्ठाष्टमभावेशौ यद्द्वावेशेत्थशालिनौ स्याताम् ॥ १५ ॥

Stanza 15: One's brother will be suffering from a dangerous disease if the lord of the 3rd is combust. The source of affliction will be in accordance with the planet who is in Ithasala with the lord of the 6th or the 8th.

पीडां तस्य प्रवदेष्ठाष्टमसंस्थिते वाऽपि ।
एवं सर्वे भाव: पित्रोस्तुयें सुते सुतानां च ॥ १६ ॥

Stanza 16: The Bhava whose lord is in the 6th or the 8th suffers affliction. In this manner should be ascertained the afflictions with reference to all Bhavas.

NOTES

Stanzas 14 to 16 underline the fact that and connection between the lord of a house and the lord of the 6th or the 8th will adversely affect the Bhava concerned. Thus if the 4th Bhava lord is connected with the lord of the 6th or the 8th, the mother will suffer; if it is the 5th Bhava lord, the children will suffer and so on. Here the point to be noted is that lord of the 6th and the 8th are first-rate malefics.

All questions pertaining to brothers, sisters short journeys and neighbours should be ascertained from the third house.

If the third is occupied by malefics, especially Mars or Rahu, there will be discord between the querent and his brothers. If the affliction is severe, the brothers will be bitter enemies.

Questions, pertaining to the disappearance of brothers and their whereabouts, should also be answered on the basis of the third house. If, for instance, a query pertains to a brother who has left the home and the lord of the 3rd is in the 8th afflicted, the brother's life may be in danger. This is one view. The other reliable view is, treat the 3rd house as the Lagna of the brother and study the events as reckoned from the 3rd. Thus if a query pertains to the profession of the brother, ascertain who the lord of the 3rd and the lord of the 10th therefrom (*i.e.*, 12th from the ascendant) are mutually disposed. An Ithasala between these two lords indicates that the brother's professional prospects are indeed bright. This method gives more accurate results. From the 3rd house can also be answered such events as to whether rumours, etc. are true or false and whether messages sent by post or otherwise will evoke response and if so the nature of such replies, etc. The first house always stands for the querent. Select the house which stands for the relative concerned (e.g., 5th for son, 9th for father, etc.) and see if there is Ithasala between the two lords. If the lords happen to be malefics, and in hostile aspect, a hostile reply or message will be received. If they are benefics but in hostile aspect, favourable response is possible after some delay. If they are benefics and the aspect is also beneficial, a favourable message can be expected without delay.

Fourth House Queries

लग्नपतिदुचतुर्थे यदि मुथशिलमथवा ग्रहे गमनम् ॥ १७ ॥
प्रष्टुः पृथ्वीलाभदमसौम्यदृग्योगतो नैव ।
यदि पृच्छति कृषिको से क्षेत्राल्लाभो भवेन्नो वा ॥ १८ ॥
लग्नं कृषिकस्तुयं भूमिर्घूनं च कृषिस्तरुर्दशमम् ।
लग्ने कुरोपगते स्याच्चौरोपद्रवस्तु कृषिकर्तुः ॥ १९ ॥

Stanza 17 to 19: If the lord of the Lagna has Muthasila with the Moon in the 4th or occupies his own house, the querent will come into possession of lands. If the combination is afflicted by malefics, contrary results will happen.

If a farmer puts the query "whether or not I will successfully cultivate a certain land" answer it thus :

The ascendant indicates the cultivator, the 4th indicates the land, the 7th rules cultivation and the

10th rules the crops. If the Lagna is occupied by a malefic, the farmer loses by theft.

वक्रातिचारवर्ज्ये क्रूरे चौरस्य कृषिलाभः
लग्नस्थे शुभखेटे साफल्यं कर्षकस्य कृषितः स्यात् ॥ २० ॥

Stanza 20: If the malefic in Lagna is free from retrogression or acceleration, the beneficiary will be the thief. If benefics are in Lagna, the farmer will benefit by cultivation.

तुर्ये च क्रूरगते त्यक्त्वा भूमिं प्रयात्येषः ।
द्यूने च शुभोपगते शुभं कृषेस्त्वन्यथा तु विपरीतम् ॥ २१ ॥

Stanza 21: If a malefic occupies the 4th, the cultivator will dispense with the land. If a benefic is located in the 7th, the cultivation will be successful. Malefics will destroy the crop.

दशमे दशमपतौ वा शुभयुतदृष्टे शुभा वृक्षाः ।
भूभाटकपृच्छायां लग्नं प्रष्टा च भाटकं द्यूने ॥ २२ ॥

तस्योत्पत्तिर्दशमे तथाऽवसानं चतुर्थं स्यात् ।
लग्नस्य लग्नपस्य च शुभयोगे शुभमशोभनं वामे ॥ २३ ॥

Stanzas 22 and 23: If the lord of the 10th is in the 10th aspected by or associated with benefics, there will be a good crop.

In a query relating to the leasing of land, the ascendant signifies the querent and the 7th indicates the, lessee, the 10th signifies the production, and the 4th rules the final profits, etc. Benefits accrue if the Lagna and its lord are connected with benefics. If they are afflicted, contrary results are shown.

घूने क्रूरोपगते यस्मादपि भाटकस्ततोऽनर्थः ।
दशमे क्रूरोपगते नोत्पत्तिर्बहुतरा भवेत्रष्टुः ॥ २४ ॥

Stanza 24: Whoever be the lessee, he will suffer if malefics are in the 7th. If the 10th is occupied by malefics, the querent will derive no benefit even if the crop yield is satisfactory.

क्रुरादिंते तु तुर्ये स्यादवसाने शुभं नास्य ॥ २४-१/२ ॥

Stanza 24½: If malefics are in the 4th, final result will be unfavourable.

NOTES

The questions dealt with in stanzas 17 to 24½ pertain to the issue of land, its acquisition, cultivation, etc, And in a sense this reflects the social conditions prevailing then. The same problems face us today also and the combinations help us to answer the question pertaining not only to land but also to other immovable property.

The fourth house represents in addition to lands mother, immovable property, hidden things, farms estates, etc.

In regard to answering questions regarding purchase of property we can regard the first house as the querent or buyer; the 7th house as the seller, the 10th house as the value or price, and the 4th the property.

If malefics are in the 4th, the buyer will not derive much benefit. If benefics are in the 10th, good revenue from the property is indicated.

If a question pertains to removal from one place to another, then the 1st, 4th and 7th signify respectively the querent, the place he is currently in, and the place he intends removing to. We can take the 10th house as representing one's business and the 4th house the place where the business is carried on. If the lord of the 10th is in Ithasala with the lord of the 7th or with the 7th, then it is better to remove the business to a new place.

The fourth house also rules conveyances. If the lords of the ascendant and the 4th are in favourable aspect, the querent is advised to buy a new car (the modern conveyance). If Mars in involved in a malefic aspect with the Lord of the 4th, the idea to purchase a new vehicle should be given up.

Lagna			
			Saturn
	Jupiter		Mercury

The query is: "Will I be successful in purchasing a certain property"?. Pisces rises and the lord of Lagna Jupiter (querent) is in Ithasala with Mercury lord of the 4th (property) and lord of the 7th (seller). The ascendant is aspected by Jupiter the lord and the 7th is occupied by the lord of the 7th. The prediction is, the querent will not only be successful but also the transaction would be smooth.

Fifth House Questions

यदि पृच्छत्येतस्याः स्त्रियो भवेन्मे प्रजा न वा कश्चित्? ॥ २५ ॥
लग्नेन्द्वोः सुतपतिना मुथशिलभावे प्रसूतिः स्यात् ।
सुतभावपतिर्लग्ने लग्नचन्द्रौ सुतेऽथवा स्याताम् ॥ २६ ॥

Stanzas 25 and 26: If a query is put "whether I will have children from this woman", the answer will be that he will have children, if the Lagna or the Moon is in Muthaseela with the lord of the 5th.

The querent will have a child early if the 5th lord is in Lagna and the lord of Lagna and the Moon are in the 5th.

सत्वरितमेव वाच्या सविसम्बे नक्तयोगेन ।
द्विशरीरे च विलग्ने शुभयुतपुत्रे द्वयपत्ययोगोऽस्ति ॥ २७ ॥

Stanza 27: If there is Nakta Yoga, the birth of issue will be delayed. If the ascendant is a dual sign and is conjoined with benefics, there will be birth of twins.

यदि लग्नपुत्रपतिः पुंराशौ चेत्स्यात्तदा सुतो गर्भे ।
पुंराशौ पुंग्रहकृतमुर्थाशलयुक्तस्तदाऽपि सुतगर्भः ॥ २८ ॥

Stanza 28: If the Lagna and the lord of the 5th are in masculine signs then a male issue will be born. If the Moon is in an odd sign and has Ithasala with a masculine planet, then also the issue will be a male.

अथवा विधुरपराह्ण सूर्यात्पृष्टे तदा स्त्री स्यात् ।
होरास्वामी पुरुषः पुंराशौ चेतथाऽपि सुतगर्भः ॥ २९ ॥

Stanza 29: Or if the query is put after midday when the Moon is behind the Sun, then the issue will be a female. If the lord of the Hora is a masculine planet and is in a male sign, a son will be born.

NOTES

The Moon will be behind the Sun from the latter part of the the 7th lunar day of the dark half of the lunar month to the New Moon.

चन्द्रयुक्तेक्षिते गर्भे सौम्ययुक्तेक्षितेऽपि वा ।
उच्चस्थेऽभ्युदिते तत्र पुण्यापत्यं प्रजायते ॥ ३० ॥

Stanza 30: If the Moon or Mercury is in the 5th or in conjunction with (or aspecting) the lord of the 5th or the lord of the 5th is exalted, the querent will get a legitimate issue.

एषा गर्भवती किल न वा प्रमाणं प्रयाति गर्भोऽयम् ? ।
प्रश्ने लग्नपशशिनो: सुतस्थयोगर्भवत्येव ॥ ३१ ॥

Stanza 31: When a query is put "whether this lady is pregnant", predict that she is pregnant if the lords of the ascendant and the Moon are in the 5th house.

यद्येतयोर्मुथशिलं केन्द्रे सुतपेन गर्भिणी तदपि ।
आपोक्लिमेत्थशालादनीक्षणाल्लग्नपुत्रयोर्नेवम् ॥ ३२ ॥

Stanza 32:—If the Moon or the lord of the ascendant is in an Apoklima in Ithasala with the ascendant or the 5th house, but aspected by the 5th lord, then the woman has not conceived.

चरलग्ने कूरेन्द्रोर्मुथशिलभावे विनश्यति हि गर्भ: ।
लग्नपशशिनोस्तत्पतिस्थवक्रिमुथशिलेऽपि तथा ॥ ३३ ॥

Stanza 33: If the ascendant is a movable sign (Chara Rasi) and a malefic occupying it is in Muthaseela with the waning Moon, or if the Lagna is Chara and the lord of the Moon occupying it is in Ithasala with a retrograde planet, the lady will have abortion.

जीवितमरणप्रश्ने बालानामन्त्यपे शुभैर्दृष्टे ।
केन्द्रस्थे सितपक्षे शुभयुक्तेऽन्त्ये विधौ जीवेत् ॥ ३४ ॥

Stanza 34: If the query is "whether the child, in the womb will die or live", say it will live if the lord of the 12th is in a Kendra in conjunction with or aspected by benefics; or if the query is put during Sukla Paksha (waning Moon) and the Moon is in the 12th conjoined with benefics, the child in the womb will live.

क्रूरश्चेदन्त्यपतिर्दग्धश्वापोक्लमेऽयुक्तः ।
क्रूरस्तु जातमात्रो म्रियते बालोऽथवा गर्भे ॥ ३५ ॥

Stanza 35: If the lord of the 12th is a malefic, is combust or is in an Apoklima not aspected by or conjoined with benefics, the child will die after birth or when in the womb.

NOTES

In the above stanza bearing on the 5th house combinations are enumerated for predicting whether one will have a male or female issue, or whether there will be miscarriage, still-birth or death immediately after birth, etc.

In our experience it has been found that when the lord of the 5th is in the ascendant or the lord of the ascendant is in the 5th unafflicted, we can predict the birth of an issue. When the 5th is afflicted by Rahu or Mars, it is an indication of barrenness. It is also advisable to calculate the Beeja Sphuta or Kshetra Sphuta according as the person whom the query concerns is a male or a female. Mars in the ascendant or the 5th in Ithasala with Saturn or Rahu indicates difficult delivery.

Bhava Prasna

प्रसवज्ञानप्रश्ने भुक्ताँल्लग्नांशकान् परित्यज्य ।
भोग्याद्रिचिन्त्य शेषाननुमित्येवं वदेद्दिवसान् ॥ ३६ ॥

Stanza 36: In a query relating to the time of delivery, the number of Navamsas passed in the Lagna signify the age of the pregnancy. The number of Navamsas remaining and the degrees remaining in the ruling Navamsa signify respectively the number of months and days yet to pass for the delivery to take place.

NOTES

Predicting the time of delivery is a difficult problem. And no foolproof method has so far been devised though some astrologers have been able to forecast the date on the basis of the conception time, as per the methods given in *Brihat Jataka* and other standard works.

Suppose at the time of question, 25° 30′ of Leo rises. This means the 8th Navamsa is rising and in the 8th 2° 10′ has passed. (7 Navamsas × 3° 20′ = 23° 20′ : 25° 30′ − 23′ 20′ = 2° 10:)

According to Tajaka, the woman is in her 8th month of pregnancy and her delivery is likely in about 2 months' time. As each Navamsa (3° 20′) is equivalent to 30 days, 2° 20′ (remaining in the 8th Navamsa) will be equal to

$$\left(\frac{30}{3° 20'} \times 2° 20' \right) = 12 \text{ days}.$$

which means she will deliver after 1 month and 12 days from the date of question. I have dealt in greater detail with the question of timing events in horary astrology in the Introduction to this Book. But the method given in this stanza does not seem to work in actual practice: it has not worked at least in the majority of cases.

मासज्ञानस्य पृच्छायां गर्भिण्याभृगुनन्दनः ॥ ३७ ॥

लग्नात्स्याद्यावति स्थाने मासानाख्याति तावतः ।
सुतारसंख्या तदा वाच्या यदा धर्मात्परं गतः ॥ ३८ ॥

Stanzas 37 and 38: The lady will deliver in so many months as the number of signs reckoned from the ascendant to the position of Venus. If Venus occupies the 10th, 11th, or 12th house, then the number of months will correspond to the number of signs from the 5th house to the position of Venus. This is the view of *Bhuvana Pradeepa*.

लग्नान्तदिन राशिर्दिवा ग्रहो लग्नपश्च दिनराशौ ।
तद्दिवसे जन्म वाच्यं विपरीते व्यत्ययश्चैषाम् ॥ ३९ ॥

Stanza 39: If the ascendant is a diurnal sign, or the query is put during the day, or the lord of the ascendant is in a dual sign, the child will be born during day time; otherwise the birth will be during night.

NOTES

By "otherwise" in the above sloka is meant, the reverse combinations viz., the ascendant being a nocturnal sign, the query being put during the night time and the ascendant lord occupying a nocturnal sign.

अथ रात्रिलग्नमह्ना तदधिपतिश्चेत्तु तस्य राशिपते: ।
बलमूह्यं दिनहोरापुंराशिस्त्रीगृहेऽप्येवम् ॥ ४० ॥

Stanza 40: If a nocturnal sign rises but the query is put during day time then the result is to be guessed on the basis of the disposition of the Lagna lord, the lord of the sign occupied by the Lagna lord, Dina Hora, etc.

NOTES

Suppose a nocturnal sign rises when the query is put during day time. The Lagna lord is the Moon (nocturnally strong.) He is also in Taurus, a nocturnal sign and its lord Venus is also in a nocturnal place. Note also the lord of Kala Hora. Weighing the relative strengths of these planets, determine whether the birth takes place during day time or night time.

As we have already said elsewhere it is not advisable to give a categorical judgment until the student has gained sufficient experience in the art of interpretation.

अस्मिन्वर्षेऽपत्यं भविता विलग्नपंचमाधीशौ ।
भजतो यदित्यशालं तत्रैवाब्दे भवति नूनम् ॥ ४१ ॥

यदि वा मिथो ग्रहगतौ स्यातामेतौ च संततिस्तदपि ।
वाच्या तस्मिन्वर्षे शुभयोगादन्यथा न पुन: ॥ ४२ ॥

सूताप्रसूतयुवतिज्ञाने सुतपीऽथ षष्ठप: सूर्यात् ।
निर्गत्योदयमायात्ततः प्रसूते च नारीयम् ॥ ४३ ॥

अथजीवसौम्यशुक्राआकाशेउदयिनस्तथाप्येवम् ॥ ४३-१/२॥

Stanzas 41 to 43½: If a query "will I get a child this year?" is put, the birth of an issue should be predicted when there is Ithasala between the lords of the first and fifth.

Birth of a child should be predicted if the lord of the 1st is in the 5th and the lord of the 5th is in the 1st subject to benefic aspects. Otherwise there will be no issue.

If the lord of the 5th or 6th being free from combustion; or Jupiter, Mercury or Venus rises in the ascendant, there will be birth of an issue.

NOTES

These 3½ stanzas call for no explanation.

Sloka 41 reads: Vilagnam panchamadheesam yadi Ithasala bhajathaha thatraivabdhe apathyam bhavathi. The issue will be born in the year in which the lord of the 1st and 5th enter Ithasala. Simply put, find when the lords of the 1st and 5th will come into a trine or sextile aspect and predict the birth of issue at that period.

Jupiter 25			
	Ascdt. 20 Mars 2		Sun 28

In the given chart, lord of the 5th Jupiter is in 25° Pisces in the 5th house and the lord of the ascendant Mars is in Scorpio 2°, the query date being 17-10-1963. It was an advanced case of pregnancy. By transit, Mars and Jupiter will be in exact trine on 17th November. In fact the delivery took place on 18th November 1963.

If at the time of question the expected time of delivery is near, then the above theory of the event taking place when the lords of the ascendant and the 5th forming Ithasala will work satisfactorily.

There is also a theory that the delivery takes place in as many months as the lord of the 5th is removed from the 5th bhava madhya each sign representing one month. The practical workability of this theory is yet to be established.

Sixth House Questions

रोगादयमुत्थास्यति नवेति लग्नं भिषक् द्यूनम् ॥ ४४ ॥

व्याधिर्दशमं रोगी हिबुकं भेषजमिहाहुराचार्याः ।
क्रूरार्दिते विलग्ने वैद्यान्नगुणस्तदौषधाद्रोगः ॥ ४५ ॥

Stanzas 44 and 45: To answer a question pertaining to disease and its cure or otherwise, consider the Lagna as signifying the physician, the seventh disease, the tenth patient and the fourth medicine or treatment. If malefics are in or aspect the ascendant, the disease cannot be cured by the physician.

वृद्धिमुपयाति दशमे क्रूरैर्निजबुद्धितोऽप्यगुणः ।
अस्ते च क्रूरयुक्ते मद्यान्मांद्यं तथौषधाद्वन्धौ ॥ ४६ ॥

Stanza 46: On the contrary, the disease, will be intensified. If malefics are in the 10th due to the querent's own fault, the treatment will not work. If malefics are in the 7th or 4th, one complication will lead to another complication.

सौम्योपगतैरेतैररोगता रोगिणो भवसि ।
लग्नेशेन्द्वौ: सौम्येत्थशालतो रोगनाशनं वाच्यम् ॥ ४७ ॥

Stanza 47: Benefics in the above places will enable the patient to get cured. If the lord of the Lagna and the Moon are in Ithasala with benefics, the disease, will be destroyed.

वक्रे तु तत्र खेटे भूयोऽपि गद: समुपयाति ।
भूमिस्थे लग्नस्थे द्यूनस्थे शशिसुथशिले भवेन्मृत्यु: ॥ ४८ ॥

Stanza 48: If the planets (lords of the above houses) are retrograde, the disease will again appear or there will be relapse. If the retrograde planets (in the 1st, 4th, 7th or 10th) are in Ithasala with the Moon, the patient will die.

NOTES

According to stanzas 45 to 48, the ascendant, the 7th, the 10th and the 4th respectively signify the physician (or surgeon), the disease (or illness), the patient and the treatment.

Malefics in the ascendant are no indication of the illness being cured. If malefics are in the 10th, the treatment will do no good due to the patient's own fault such as incorrect dieting, etc. If the affliction is centered on the 4th and 7th, then complications set in. Benefics will enable the patient to get relief. But if they are retrograde, after some signs of recovery, the patient will have a relapse. And if the malefics are in Ithasala with the Moon, death will result.

Disease is assigned to 7th house. But in our humble opinion, the 6th house should be considered as signifying disease and the judgment should be made on the basis of the ascendant, its lord, planets in it, the 6th house, the lord of the 6th and the planets in the 6th and the Yogas caused between these two sets of factors. If the concerned factors, e.g., the ascendant lord or the lord of the 6th is in a movable sign, the patient becomes relieved soon; if the sign is fixed, it will be a long disease. If the sign is common, illness will be neither long nor short.

If the lord of the ascendant is in the 6th and the lord of the 6th in the ascendant, the patient has to suffer a lot and for a long time too. If the 6th and 8th lords are both in the ascendant, death ensues. If the lords of the 6th and 8th interchange, there will be speedy recovery. These observations are due to our own studies and, therefore, the readers need not take them as quite authoritative.

लग्नस्थे रन्ध्रपतौ लग्नशपशिनोविनाशे वा ।
लग्नाधिपे च सूर्ये चन्द्रः सप्तेशसुशिलविधायी ॥ ४९ ॥

सप्तेशे षष्ठस्थे तन्मरणं रोगिणो वाच्यम् ।
रंध्रेशेन विनष्टेनास्तमितेनापि केन्द्रस्थे ॥ ५० ॥

लग्नेश च मुथशिले मृत्युः स्याद्रोगपृच्छायाम् ।
अथ वा तयोश्च केन्द्रे मुथशिलतः क्रूरपीडिते मरणम् ॥ ५१ ॥

Stanzas 49 to 51: The patient dies under the following combinations: (a) Lord of the 8th occupies the ascendant; (b) lord of the ascendant or lord of the 8th is in the 8th house from the Moon; (c) the Sun is lord of Lagna and the Moon causes Ithasala with the lord of the 7th posited in the 6th; (d) there is Ithasala between the lord of the 8th; or the ascendant lord occupying a quadrant, and a planet in combustion or retrogression; and (e) the lord of Lagna and the 8th occupy afflicted quadrants and there is Ithasala between these two lords.

NOTES

Combination (c) can happen only when the Prasna Lagna or the sign rising at the time of query is Leo or Simha.

According to combination (d) either the lord of the 8th or the lord of the ascendant should be in a quadrant having Ithasala with a planet who is retrograde or combust.

सूर्यद्वादशभागं प्रविष्टे लग्नेश्वरेऽप्येवम् ।
लग्ने चरे च रोगो क्षणे स्यादरुक् सरुक्चापि ॥ ५२ ॥

Stanza 52: If the ascendant is in the Dwadasamsa of the Sun the patient dies. If the ascendant falls in a movable sign (Chara Rasi) the patient appears to recover but again there will be a relapse.

NOTES

For the disease to come under control for a while but aggravate again, the Lagna must be a movable sign and the lord of Lagna must occupy the Dwadasamsa of the Sun.

द्विशरीरे पररोग: स्थिरे गदस्यव रोगत्वम् ।
शशिनो वक्रमुथशिले स्थिररोगो मंदमुथशिले पूर्वम् ॥ ५३ ॥

Stanza 53: If the ascendant is a common sign, the disease will be other than the suspected one. If the ascendant is in a fixed sign, the disease is as suspected.

If the Moon is in Muthaseela with a retrograde planet, it will be a chronic disease.

NOTES

This stanza enables us to judge whether or not the patient suffers from the suspected disease and whether or not it is a chronic complaint.

The rising sign must be a common sign if the disease is to be other than the one originally suspected. If the Lagna is a fixed sign, the preliminary diagnosis is correct. The complaint is chronic if the Moon has Ithasala with a retrograde planet.

मूत्रनिरोधाद्रोगोत्पत्तिर्ज्ञेयाकृतप्रश्ने ।
अथ पृच्छायाः पूर्वे सप्ताहानि च विलोक्य चत्वारि ॥ ५४ ॥

यदि तेषु शशिकवि शुभयुतदृष्टौ तदा शस्तम् ।
मंदोऽयमथ नवेति प्रश्ने लग्नेश्वरोऽथ चन्द्रो वा ॥ ५५ ॥

षष्ठेशमुथशिलो स्यादस्तमितो वा तदा मन्दः ॥ ५५-१/२ ॥

Stanzas 54 and 55½: If the Moon's Muthaseela is with a slow-moving planet, the disease first originated from the blocking of the urinary passage. If on the 4th or 7th day prior to the query, the Sun and the Moon were subject to benefic influences, the patient will recover. The illness will continue if the lord of the ascendant or the Moon has Ithasala with the lord of the 6th, or is combust.

NOTES

Since the Moon is the fastest moving of all the other planets, 'slow moving' under stanza 54 can only refer to Saturn, though some commentators opine that it could be any superior planet (Mars, Jupiter or Saturn).

Several cases of urine-suppression, and prostate-gland trouble reveal the hand of Saturn. If is therefore reasonable to say that if the Moon has Ithasala with Saturn-involving the 6th house-the source of trouble will be the urinary passage.

The latter half of stanza 54—the Sun and the Moon having benefic aspects on the 4th or 7th day prior to the query date is not very clear, but it occurs to me that planets in certain aspects prior to putting the query will have given rise to the illness or aggravated it. This theory merits serious attention of all astrological students.

I should like to make a few general observations based on my experience. All questions regarding sickness, disease, etc., are signified by the 6th house and to some extent by the 8th house too.

Stanza 45 says that the patient is denoted by the 10th house (dasamam rogee). I feel that the ascendant, its lord, the Moon and the planets which afflict them (affliction according to Tajaka rules) are the main indicators of the sick person. The part of the body affected will be either (a) the part signified by the house the lord of the ascendant is in, (b) the part signified by the sign the Moon is in, (c) or the part signified by the sign the lord of the 6th house is in.

Benefics in the 6th show speedy recovery. The sickness is a complicated one if the 6th or its lord is involved in any 'Yoga' with 8th or 12th (or their lords).

If the ascendant is strong, the disease is a passing phase. Adverse aspects between the lords of the ascendant and the 8th denotes death. In many cases of long illness, the ascendant lord is found in the 6th and the 6th lord in the ascendant. If the ascendant lord is in Bhavishya Ithasala (applying aspect) with the lord of the 6th, the illness will continue until the Yoga is cleared. The illness can hardly be cured if the lords of the 6th and ascendant are in mutual association or aspect. The illness may fatally end if the lord of the ascendant is in the 8th with Mars or there is 'Gairakamboola' of Mars in a mutual aspect between the lords of the ascendant and the 8th

As the sick-man already knows what his health trouble is, it will be of service to him if he is informed whether or not his illness is serious and when he will recover.

Different houses govern different organs and the diseases appearing therein. For details reference may be made to the chapter on "Medical Astrology in our book *Hindu Predictive Astrology*. For ready reference, the following information is given about house and the significations.

First house—head, brain and nerve centres; second house—face, throat, neck and gullet; third house—the shoulders, arms, chest, lungs, breath and nerves; fourth house—the breast and stomach; fifth house—back, heart, liver and blood: sixth house—bowels, waist, intestines and liver; seventh—kidneys; eighth—rectum, sexual organs, spine, excretary system and bladder; ninth—arterial system, the thighs and hips; tenth—knees, bones and joints; eleventh—ankles and breath; and twelfth—the feet. the lymphatic system and the eyes.

In the allocation of organs, there is some difference amongst different writers. We would for instance allocate the eyes to the 2nd and the 12th.

According to the famous classical work *Krishneeya*, if malefics aspect or occupy the 6th and 8th house. the patient will never recover from his sick-bed. If both benefics and malefics influence these two places, the recovery will be slow and delayed. If the ascendant lord is in a trine and the 9th house is aspected by a benefic, he will recover after treatment. If the 9th house is occupied by a benefic, no recovery is possible. If benefics are in the 6th and 8th or benefics aspect these two houses, then the querent has no illness.

		Venus 23	Mercury 16
		21-7-1961 at 8-23 a.m. (I.S.T.) at Bangalore	Sun 6
Jupiter 10 Saturn 4-30			Ascendant 10 Mars 21
		Moon 8	

Here is a question: "Will the patient recover?" Lord of the ascendant is in the 12th in Easarapha with Saturn lord of the 6th (illness). 7th (a maraka) and Jupiter lord of the 8th (death), The affliction is in the 6th house-serious affliction to liver. The patient's urinary passage had been blocked. The prediction was given that he will not survive. He was operated and died immediately after operation.

Employer-Employee Relations

ईशोऽन्यो मम भविता न वेति लग्नेश्वरस्य यदि केन्द्रे ॥ ५६ ॥

नो भवति मुथशिलं षष्ठान्त्यपतिभ्यां तदा नान्यः ।
वक्री वाऽन्येन समं लग्नपतिः सहजनवमसंस्थेन ॥ ५७ ॥

कुरुते यदित्थशालं तदाऽन्यनाथो भवेत्प्रष्टुः ।
लग्नपतौ केन्द्रस्थे रिपुदृष्ट्या क्रूरवीक्षिते पुण्ये ॥ ५८ ॥

रविरश्मिगतेऽथ भवेद्यावज्जीवं च नान्यपतिः ॥ ५८-१/२ ॥

Stanzas 56 to 58½: A query like "will I serve another master?" should be answered thus: If the lord of the ascendant is in a quadrant having no Muthaseela with the lord of the 6th or 12th, there will be no change of service. If the lord of the ascendant is retrograde and is in Ithasala with a planet in the 3rd or 9th, the querent will change over to a new master. If the lord of the ascendant is in a quadrant and is aspected adversely by a malefic and the *Punyasaham* is combust, then there will be no change of the master throughout the life of the querent.

NOTES

In the above slokas combinations are given for predicting whether one would change his master. The master-servant relations do not hold good in the modern world when the labour class can assert its rights and dictate terms. Such questions as "whether one would change service etc., can be answered on the basis of the above stanzas.

One will change service, *i.e.*, seek a position under a new proprietor or management under the following combinations:

(a) Lord of the ascendant in the 1st, 4th, 7th or 10th having no Ithasala with the lord of the 6th or 12th.

(b) The ascendant lord in the 1st, 4th, 7th or 10th, adversely aspected (square or opposition) by a malefic and the *Punyasaham* is combust.

Change of job can be predicted when the lord is retrograde and has Ithasala with 3rd or 9th.

According to Tajaka writers, the 3rd and 9th houses indicate change—change of position, change of place, etc.

अयमीशो भद्रो मे पृच्छायां लग्नपस्य कंबूले ॥ ५९ ॥

स्वामी स एव भव्यो द्यूनेशस्य च शुभोऽन्येशः ।
गृहभूमिस्थानानां लग्नप्रश्ने पुरोक्त एव विधिः ॥ ६० ॥

सम्यग्विचार्य वाच्यं शुभमशुभं पृच्छतः स्वधिया ॥ ६०-१/२ ॥

Stanzas 59 to 60½: A query such as "will my interests be safe under the present master?"—should be answered thus: If the lord of Lagna is in Kamboola Yoga with the Moon, then the querent's interests are safe under the present master. If the Kamboola Yoga is between the lord of the 7th and the Moon it is better to serve under a new master. In a similar manner, queries bearing on lands, houses, leases, etc., should be answered by a proper assessment of the favourable and unfavourable factors.

भृत्यचतुष्पदलाभप्रश्ने लग्नेशशीतगू षष्ठे ।
षष्ठेशमुथशिलौ वा लग्ने षष्ठेश्वरोऽथ तल्लाभः ॥ ६१ ॥

Stanza 61: In queries as to whether one would get a servant or cattle: if the lord of the ascendantand the Moon are in the 6th or the Lagna lord has Ithasala with the lord of the 6th, or if the lord of the 6th is in the ascendant, the querent will get servants and cattle.

Seventh House Questions

स्त्रीलाभस्य प्रश्ने स्मराधिपे लग्नपेन शशिना वा ॥ ६२ ॥

कृतमुथशिले युवत्या अयाचितया भवेल्लाभः ।
यदि लग्नपो विधुर्वा द्यूने तद्याचितां स्त्रियं लभते ॥ ६३ ॥

Stanzas 62 and 63: In a query about marriage, if the lord of the 7th is in Ithasala with the lord of the ascendant or the Moon, the querent gets a bride without his seeking. If the lord of the Lagna or the Moon is in the 7th, then the bride is secured with effort.

लग्नेशान्मूसरिफे चन्द्रस्तपमुथशिले स्वयं लाभः ।
येन समं तु मुथशिलस्तत्र विनष्टे च पापयुतदृष्टे ॥ ६४ ॥

निकटीभूय तद् किल विनश्यति स्त्रीगतं कार्यम् ।
पापेऽत्र रन्ध्रनाथे स्त्रीजातेरेव विघटते कार्यम् ॥ ६५ ॥

सहजपतौ भ्रातृभ्यस्तुर्येशे पितृत एव नान्येभ्यः ।
सौम्यकृतयुतिदृग्भ्यां पूर्वोक्तस्थानतः शुभं वाच्यम् ॥ ६६ ॥

Stanzas 64 to 66: If the lord of the ascendant is in Musaripha with the Moon or in Ithasala with the lord of the 7th, the querent secures a bride without effort. If the planet with whom Ithasala is caused is in combustion or afflicted by malefics, the querent will not succeed in getting a bride. If the lord of the 8th is a malefic the object of securing a bride will be defeated. According as the 3rd or 4th lord happens to be a malefic, the failure (in securing a bride) will be due respectively to the brothers and father. If in the chart, combinations are affected by benefic planets, the object will be realised through the appropriate sources.

NOTES

The five stanzas given above bear on the success or failure of a querent in securing a bride.

The querent will be able to get a bride without his having to try when (a) the lord of the ascendant (or the Moon) and the 7th lord are in Ithasala; (b) when the ascendant lord and the Moon are in Musaripha.

His efforts to secure a bride will be successful provided the Moon or the ascendant lord is in the 7th.

If the lord of the 7th (with whom the ascendant lord causes Ithasala) is conjoined by malefics, or is combust the querent faces failure. Similar will be the case if the lord of the 8th is malefic. The source of failure will be the brother or father according as the lord of the 3rd or 4th is a malefic. If benefics are also involved, then through these very sources, the querent will be successful in finding a bride.

Musaripha, Ithasala, etc., have been fully described in my book *Varshaphal* and briefly in the last chapter of this book. According to Stanza 66, the 4th signifies father, but we feel that the 9th should be considered.

प्रीतिस्थानप्रश्ने स्मरपतिलग्नेशमुथशिले स्नेहः ।
झकटकदृशा झकटकः शशिकंबूले तु साऽपि शुभा ॥ ६७ ॥

Stanza 67: In regard to a query bearing on love affairs, say there will be friendship and love if the lord of the ascendant is in Muthaseela with the lord of the 7th. If these two lords are in hostile aspect, the couple will always quarrel. If either lord has Kamboola Yoga with the Moon, the bride will be endowed with character.

यदि मन्दो लग्नेशः केन्द्रे च स्यात्तदा बली प्रष्टा ।
अस्तेश्वरे च मन्दे केन्द्रे प्रतिवादिनोऽस्ति बलम् ॥ ६८ ॥

Stanza 68: According as Saturn happening to be lord of the ascendant or the 7th occupies a Kendra, the querent or the bride will have the upper hand.

उभयोरेकस्थितयोर्ज्ञातव्या झकटकं तयोः प्रीतिः ।
सूर्ये न शुभं विबले नरस्य शुक्रे स्त्रियो द्वयोर्द्वितयौ ॥ ६९ ॥

Stanza 69: If both the planets are in the same sign, infer that the couple will quarrel but become reconciled. According as the Sun, Venus or both are weak, the bridegroom or bride or both the couple will lack happiness.

NOTES

The combinations given in stanzas 67 to 69 can very well be used for answering questions pertaining to disputes, partnerships, friendships, etc. The ascendant represents the plaintiff, appellant or the querent and the 7th signifies the defendant or the partner or the opponent.

Stanza 67 can be applied for predicting compromise or continuation of mutual hostility. Stanza 68 can be used in predicting whether the plaintiff or defendant will have the upper hand.

For a querent to win in a dispute, the lord of the 7th must be weak occupying the 6th while the lord of the ascendant must be strong and beneficially disposed.

मम गृहिणी रुष्टा पुनरेष्यति नो वाऽथ भूम्यधःस्थरवौ ।
भूपरिगते च शुक्रे नैति पुनर्वक्रितेऽभ्येति ॥ ७० ॥

सूर्यान्निर्गतशुक्रे वक्रेऽपि समेति चान्यथा रुष्टा ।
क्षीणेन्दौ बहुदिवसैः पूर्णविधौ च द्रुतमुपैति ॥ ७१ ॥

Stanzas 70 and 71: If the query "whether my angry wife will return home" is put, say that she will not return if the Sun is in the 1st, 2nd or 3rd house, and Venus is in the 5th, 6th or 7th. If Venus is either retrograde or is heliacally rising, the wife will return. If Venus is not retrograde or is combust, the wife will not return. She will return after considerable delay or early according as the Moon is waning or waxing.

NOTES

The couple quarrel and the wife leaves the husband. He wants to know whether or not she would return back to him.

She will not return (a) if the Sun is in houses prior to the 4th and Venus is in the houses 5, 6 and 7; (b) she will return if Venus has left combustion or is retrograde; (c) she will return after a lapse of time if the Moon is waning; and (d) she will return early if the Moon is waxing.

The following observations based on my experience are for the guidance of the readers:—

Whether it is the wife or the husband that puts the question, the 1st house signifies the querent and the 7th the partner. We can safely predict that a married couple living separately at the time of query will live again together if the lord of the ascendant is in the 7th unafflicted or the lords of the ascendant and the 7th are in mutual favourable aspect. The retrograde positions of the two lords do not favour reconciliation. On the other hand, if one of the lords is retrograde, the person signified by the lord (*e.g.*, 7th-wife) will be recalcitrant but they will come together if the aspect is favourable.

Questions bearing on divorce can also be answered under the above combinations. Lords of the 1st and 7th in mutual evil aspect and afflicted by Rahu or Mars is an indication of impending divorce. If the two lords are in mutual evil aspect but conjoined by Jupiter or Venus, the desire for divorce will give place to the desire for reconciliation. If the Lagna lord is afflicted by Mars or Rahu, the querent is desirous of divorce. If the 7th lord is afflicted, then the partner will try for divorce. Even if legal proceedings are going on, the couple will drop the idea of divorce if the ascendant lord, being retrograde, is aspected by Jupiter or Venus.

एषा कुमारिका किल निर्दोषा किन्न वेति पृच्छायाम् ।
लग्ने स्थिरे स्थिरर्क्षे लग्नपशशिनोश्च निर्दोषा ॥ ७२ ॥

Stanza 72: If a question is put: "Is the bride pure in her character", say she is pure if the ascendant is a fixed sign and the lord of the ascendant and the Moon are also in fixed signs.

चरराशिगतैरेतैरियं कुमार्यपि च जातदोषा स्यात् ।
द्विशरीरस्थे चन्द्रे चरलग्ने स्वल्पदोषा स्यात् ॥ ७३ ॥

Stanza 73: If the ascendant, the ascendant lord and the Moon are in movable signs, the girl's character will not be pure. If the Moon is in a common sign and the ascendant is a movable sign, the girl's character will be suspicious.

NOTES

In answering questions pertaining to the sexual purity or otherwise of a girl, great care should be taken, especially in India, where despite the cry of some "social-minded women", the virginity of a girl is a *sine-qua-non* of all other considerations. The slightest astrological suggestion, often based upon an inadequate consideration of all the astrological factors involved, will often have a most serious repercussion on the future of the girl and her family. The above two combinations, based merely on the nature-movable, fixed or common-of a sign rising or the sign occupied by the ascendant lord and the Moon, are not the exclusive factors to give correct finding.

In many questions dealt with by me, I have found Mars and Venus in evil aspect to the seventh or the lord of the ascendant. If instead of Mars, Rahu joins Venus, the bride may have been tempted but she will not be unchaste. In any case, it is not desirable to make a categorical prediction so far as a woman's character is concerned. Jupiter's aspect always nullifies any affliction.

शशिभौमावेकर्क्षे स्थिरवर्जे तत्परेण गुप्तमियम्
रमिता शनिचन्द्रमसोलँग्नगयोः प्रकटमुपभुक्ता ॥ ७४ ॥

Stanza 74: If the Moon and Mars are in movable or common sign, the girl will have committed adultery in secret. If the Moon and Saturn are in Lagna, her sexual impurity will be an open secret.

यदि भौमशनी केन्द्रे विधुदृष्टे वृश्चिकेऽथ शुक्रः स्यात् ।
तद्द्रेष्काणेऽथ तदा निर्भ्रान्तं जातदोवैषा ॥ ७५ ॥

Stanza 75: The girl will be definitely guilty of adultery if Mars and Saturn occupy a quadrant aspected by the Moon and if Venus occupies the Drekkana of the Moon.

NOTES

The stanzas are simple enough not needing any explanations. As we have said in our notes under stanzas 72 and 73, a categorical judgment about the character of a bride or bridegroom should not be given. In Western countries where the sanctity attached to chastity before marriage has been fast disappearing, the bride or even the bridegroom may not bother much. But there are also certain families in the West who continue to entertain conservative views in such matters and where only virgin brides are preferred.

एषा किल प्रसूता सिते घटे ज्ञे हरौ च नो सूता ।
अनयोरलिवृषगतयोः सूता नारी परिज्ञेया ॥ ७६ ॥

Stanza 76: The woman will not yet have delivered if Venus is in Aquarius and Mercury is in Leo. If

Venus and Mercury are in Scorpio and Taurus, the delivery will have already taken place.

NOTES

The above combinations require the situation of Mercury and Venus in the 7th from each other which is an impossibility. Hence their situation together in one of the four signs should be considered.

भौमबुधशुक्रचन्द्रा द्विशरीरे चापवर्जिते चेत्स्युः ।
अग्रेऽस्ति तत्प्रसूतिश्चापे नाग्रे न पृष्ठतः सूता ॥ ७७ ॥

Stanza 77: If Mars, Mercury, Venus and the Moon are in common signs (except Sagittarius) the lady will deliver early. If they are in Sagittarius, the delivery will not take place.

क्रूरश्चेच्चरराशौ परतः सूता स्थिरे तु निजपत्युः ।
मिश्रे तु मिश्रमूह्यं जातकसन्देहपृच्छायाम् ॥ ७८ ॥

Stanza 78: If malefics are in movable signs, the pregnancy will be due to a person other than the father. If the malefics are in fixed signs, the child is born to the father. If mixed influences prevail, the fatherhood remains questionable.

NOTES

If a question is put: "whether the conception is legitimate or illegitimate, i.e., due to the husband or to a lover or outsider" then we have to predict the legitimacy or otherwise on the basis of the above three stanzas. Here also the readers are cautioned not to make any judgment, lest the repercussions on the life of the couple be adverse.

It has been found that when the lord of the ascendant (or the Moon) is in favourable aspect with the lord of the 11th, the issue in conception is legitimate. When the aspect is adverse, and is further afflicted by Saturn or Mars, the child is illegitimate. It may also stated that the affliction or otherwise of the 5th lord also gives a clue.

		Ascendant	
			Sun Venus
Saturn	Jupiter		

In this chart pertaining to a question put to the author, on the legitimacy of the issue in conception, lords of the ascendant and 11th, viz., Venus and Jupiter are in trines unafflicted. The finding was, it was a legitimate conception.

गुर्विण्येषा पत्युः परपुरुषाद्वेति लग्नसुतपत्योः ।
शुभयुतिदृग्भ्यां स्वपतेः शनिभौमदृशाऽन्यतो गुर्वी ॥ ७९ ॥

Stanza 79: A question such as "Is this woman's conception due to her husband or another person" should be answered thus. The conception is due to the husband if the lords of the ascendant and the 5th are aspected by or conjoined with benefics; if aspected by Saturn and Mars, it is due to another person

कुलटा सतीयमथवा लग्नपतिश्चन्द्रमाश्च भोमेन ।
एकांशे मुथशिलकृत्तदैव भवने भजत्यन्यम् ॥ ८० ॥

Stanza 80: "Is this woman a Kulata (harlot) or a Sati (a devoted wife)" be the question, she may be considered to have committed adultery in her own house if the lord of the ascendant or the Moon is in degree conjunction with Mars.

यदि निजगृहगो भौमस्तदाऽन्यदेशं प्रयाति जारकृते ।
रविणेति मुथशिले सत्युपभुक्ता सा तु राजपुरुषेण ॥ ८१ ॥

Stanza 81: If Mars is in his own sign, then she will have committed the sin in another's house. If the Sun is in Muthasila with Mars, her intimacy is with a high personage.

सौम्येन लेखकदणिङ्‌निजभे शुक्रेण योषयेव स्त्री ।
एतैर्योगैरसती विपरीते सुचरितेति विज्ञेयम् ॥ ८२ ।

Stanza 82: If Mars has Muthasila with Mercury, her parmour is a trader or a writer. If Mars has Muthasila with Venus, then she will be guilty of homosexuality. If contrary combinations exist, the lady will be pure in character.

लग्नपतिनाऽथ शशिना मूसरिफे भूसुते भवेज्जार: ।
युक्त: पुनर्गुरुदृशा पुत्रभयाद्रविदृशा च राजभयात् ॥ ८३ ॥
सितदृष्ट्या परनारी भयात्सितज्ञैकराशिगतदृष्ट्या ।
जारस्य स्थविरत्वाल्लज्जितात्पतति जारं सा ॥ ८४ ॥

Stanzas 83 and 84: If Mars (in the above combinations) has Musaripha Yoga with the lord of the ascendant or the Moon, the lover of the woman will be to her liking. According as Mars is aspected by Jupiter, the Sun or Venus, she will be restrained by the fear of her son, or the law or other women. If Mercury and Venus together aspect Mars, she will be afraid of the scandal that her lover is an old man.

NOTES

Planet Mars is generally associated with sexual morality. Questions bearing on character should not be answered categorically lest a little slip in assessing the combinations may often lead to incorrect inferences and may consequently have dangerous repercussion on the family.

Stanzas 80 to 84 are intended to ascertain whether a woman is a chaste wife or has extra-marital relations. Stanza 79 gives combinations for judging whether an issue in conception is legitimate or illegitimate.

The woman will be guilty of adultery under the following configurations:—

(a) Ascendant lord or the Moon in *degree conjunction with* Mars.

(b) Mars occupying his own sign in Muthasila with the Sun—the lover is a high (political) personage.

(c) Mars (in *b*) in Muthasila with Mercury—the lover is a writer, journalist, novelist trader or a businessman.

(d) Mars (in *b*) in Muthasila with Venus—the parmour is a woman. Here homosexuality is implied.

(e) Mars (in *b*) in Musaripha with the Moon or ascendant lord—the lover will be to the liking of the woman.

(f) Mars (in *b*) aspected by Jupiter—the woman's amorous adventures restrained by the fear of her son.

(g) Mars (in *b*) aspected by the Sun—she is afraid of the law that she may be hauled up for prostitution.

(h) Mars (in *b*) aspected by Venus—she is afraid of scandals being spread by other women.

(i) Mars (in *b*) aspected by Mercury and Venus together occupying the same sign—she is afraid of her sin being divulged because she has liaison with an old man.

The various combinations have to be suitably assessed and balance before a conclusion is arrived at. Sexual immorality is the bane of Western countries and in this respect despite the loosening of traditional values, due not a little to the zeal of "social reformers" Indian women by and large are scrupulously moral, keeping as their ideal such hallowed women as Savitri, Seetha, etc.

Eighth House Questions

नृपसंग्रामप्रश्ने विलग्नलग्नेशसंस्थितात्खेटात् ।
शशिमूसरिफात्प्रष्टाऽस्तास्तपसंस्थेन्दुमुथशिलाच्छत्रुः ॥ ८५ ॥

Stanza 85: In regard to a question bearing on war, if the planet in the ascendant or the planet occupying the sign held by the ascendant lord is in Musaripha with the Moon the querent ruler will win. If the Moon has Muthasila with the planet in the 7th or the planet who is in the sign occupied by the lord of the 7th, the enemy will win.

अथवा शनिकुजजीवाः शीघ्रेभ्यो बलयुता उपरिचराः ।
बुधसितचन्द्रास्तेभ्यश्च दुर्बलाधश्चराश्च संचिन्त्याः ॥ ८६ ॥

Stanza 86: If superior planets are strongly placed ahead of the inferior planets or if the inferior planets being weak are behind the major planets, victory goes to the querent.

NOTES

The superior planets are Mars, Jupiter and Saturn. Astronomically though only Venus and Mercury are the inferior planets, in the context of astrology, the Moon is also an inferior planet. Stanza 86 requires (a) strong Mars, Jupiter and Saturn are so placed that they occupy signs in advance of Mercury, Venus and the Moon; (b) and weak Moon, Mercury and Venus are so placed that they are behind the superior planets.

लग्नपतावस्तपतेः षट्त्रिदशायमुथशिले द्वयोः स्नेहः ।
वर्गद्वयमध्येऽधः पतितः सोऽन्येन वध्यः स्यात् ॥ ८७ ॥

Stanza 87: If the lord of the Lagna forms Muthasila with the lord of the 7th in the 6th, 3rd, 10th or 11th, warring rulers will cease fighting by mutual agreement. If the ascendant lord is in between the ascendant and the 7th, the querent ruler will get killed in the battlefield.

वर्गद्वयाधिपानां मूसरिफेऽस्तंगतेन रणदैर्ध्यम् ।
लग्नस्वामिनि मन्दे कम्बूले उपरिगे जयः प्रष्टुः ॥ ८८ ॥

Stanza 88: If the lords of Lagna and the 7th are in Musaripha and one of the lords is combust, the war will drag on for a long time. If the lord of the ascendant being a slow-moving planet (Saturn) is in

Kamboola Yoga (with the Moon) and is ahead of a fastmoving planet, the querent will win.

NOTES

The latter half of the stanza may also be translated thus: If the lord of Lagna has Kamboola with Saturn.

एवं गुणे तु तस्मिन्विप्रविनष्टेऽस्तपतिनीचस्थे ।
केन्द्रैऽस्ते वाऽस्तपती प्रष्टुर्हानि: प्रवक्तव्या ॥ ८९ ॥

Stanza 89: If the lord of Lagna (as in stanza 88) is combust, or occupies the debilitation sign of the 7th lord or is in a quadrant from the 7th lord, or is in the 7th, the querent faces danger of defeat.

NOTES

The ascendant lord who has caused Musaripha should be combust and occupy the debilitation place of the lord of the 7th, or a Kendra to make the querent get defeated. The original reads—Asthapathi neechasthe—i.e., "the lord of the 7th must be debilitated" but the commentator interprets this part of the stanza as "the ascendant lord occupying the sign in which the lord of the 7th gets debilitated". Since the result is defeat for the querent, and victory for the enemy, the lord of the 7th should be strong and the ascendant lord weak.

लग्नादध: शुभे सति उपरि च मन्दे शुभ: सहाय: स्यात् ।
लग्नपतौ रन्ध्रस्थे रन्ध्रपतिमुथशिले मृति: प्रष्टु: ॥ ९० ॥

Stanza 90: If benefics are behind the ascendant and slow-moving planets are forwards of the ascendant, the querent gets the help of a noble person. If the lord of the ascendant is in the 8th and in Muthasila with the lord of the 8th, the querent dies in battle.

सप्तेशे धनसंस्थे धनेशकृतमुथशिले रिपोर्नाशः ।
लग्नेशदशमपत्योर्मुथशिलतः पृच्छकस्य जयवीर्यें ॥ ९१ ॥

Stanza 91: The enemy will be routed when the lord of the 7th is in the 2nd and is in Muthasila with the lord of the 2nd. The lord of the ascendant in Muthasila with the lord of the 10th indicates success to the querent.

तुर्यास्तपयोरेवं शत्रोर्योगे जयो ज्ञेयः ।
उभयवर्गोऽपि केन्द्रे तत्पतिकृतमुथशिले बलं ज्ञेयम् ॥ ९२ ॥

Stanza 92: Lords of the 4th and 7th in conjunction denotes victory to the enemy. If the lords of the ascendant and the 7th are in Kendras and in mutual Ithàsala, predict success to the party signified by the stronger of the two lords.

चरराशौ सबलत्वं जित्वा प्रान्ते विनाशस्तु ।
लग्नपतावन्त्यस्थे प्रष्टा नश्यति परोऽस्तपे षष्ठे ॥ ९३ ॥

Stanza 93: If the stronger lord, suggested in stanza 92, is in a movable sign, the party it indicates will have initial success followed by utter defeat. If the lord of the ascendant is in the 12th, the querent's army suffers losses. If the lord of the 7th is in the 6th, the enemy's army will suffer losses.

खपतौ लग्ने प्रष्टुस्तुर्येशेऽस्ते रिपोः सहायबलम् ।
यन्मुथशिलौ रवीन्दू तस्य बलं मुसरिफे हानिः ॥ ९४ ॥

Stanza 94: According as the lord of the 10th is in the ascendant or the lord of the 4th is in the 7th, the querist's or the enemy's armies will get help. The nature of help will be in accordance with the planet involved in Muthasila with the Sun or the Moon. If there is Musaripha, harm alone can befall.

NOTES

The stanzas are clear enough not requiring any detailed explanation. The victory goes to the party signified by the stronger of the two lords—ascendant lord for the querent and the lord of the 7th for the enemy.

Defeat and victory—whether in a war, dual litigation—comes under the 7th house as it represents the opposition. It is not clear why Nilakantha has dealt with these events under the eighth house, unless the fact weighed with him that the eighth being the house of destruction would be more appropriate for such matters.

Ninth House Questions

मम गमनं भविता किं नवेति लग्नेश्वरे न वा केन्द्रे ।
नवमेशमुथशिले सति नवमेशे वा भवेद्गमनम् ॥ ९५ ॥

Stanza 95: If the query put is: "Will I undertake a journey", say the querent will go. on a journey if the lord of the ascendant is. posited in a quadrant and has Muthasila with the lord of the 9th and *vice versa*.

NOTES

A contemplated journey will be undertaken when either of the following two combinations is present:—

(1) The lord of the Lagna posited in a quadrant has Muthasila with the lord of the 9th.

(2) The lord of the 9th posited in a quadrant has Muthasila with the lord of the ascendant.

The 9th house generally signifies distant travels. and pilgrimages and a mutually favorable disposition between the lords of the 1st and 9th is an indication of realisation.

लग्नस्थे नवसपतौ लग्नाधिपमुथशिले च सञ्चारात् ।
रहितो याति, पुनर्ना नवसदृशा वजिते योगे ॥ ९६ ॥

Stanza 96: If the lord of the 9th is in the ascendant and has Muthasila with the ascendant lord, there will be no journey. In the absence of a trinal aspect in the above combinations, there will be no journey.

NOTES

When the lord of the 9th is in the ascendant and has Muthasila with the ascendant Lord, there will be no journey. If there is a trinal aspect the querent will undertake a journey. Suppose the ascendant is Sagittarius and the lord of the 9th the Sun is in 2° in the ascendant and the ascendant lord Jupiter is in 9° Leo. There are both Muthasila and a trinal aspect. Consequently, a journey will be undertaken.

लग्नता केन्द्रस्थे सहजग्रहमुथशिले च विक्रूरे ।
गमनं स्यादस्मिन्वा केन्द्रे क्रूरे च नास्ति गतिः ॥ ९७ ॥

Stanza 97: If the lord of the ascendant occupying a quadrant is in Muthasila with a planet in the 3rd house and devoid of malefic aspects, there will be journey. If malefics are in Kendras, the journey will not take place.

अस्ते क्रूरेऽपि च यत्कार्यं निर्यांति विलमत एव ।
आकाशास्थे पापे राजकुलाज्ञ्येष्ठतो निजाद्वाऽपि ॥ ९८ ॥

Stanza 98: Malefics in the 7th indicate failure in the object of the journey. Malefics in the 10th indicate that the object of the journey will fail due to the Government or elders in the family.

नवमेशे मुथशिलगे लग्नाधीशेन पापरिपुदृष्टे ।
गमनेऽवसानतः स्थात्रष्टुः कष्टं क्षयोऽर्थस्य ॥ ९९ ॥

Stanza 99: If there is Muthasila between the lords of the Lagna and the 9th and malefics aspect them, the querent will meet with physical danger and loss of money in the journey.

लग्नेशे नवमेशे मुथशिलकृति रन्ध्रसप्तमे कष्टम् ।
उदये यस्मिन्यायाद्विनिःसृतिः स्यात्सुखकरः पन्थाः ॥ १०० ॥

Stanza 100: If the Muthasila between the lords of the ascendant and the 9th has reference to the 8th and 7th houses, there will be affliction during the journey. If the Yoga is in the ascendant, the querent will have a comfortable journey.

लग्नान्मार्गानुभवो व्योम्नः कार्यं स्मराद्गदिस्थानम् ।
भूमेः कार्य परिणतिरेवं लग्ने शरीरसुखम् ॥ १०१ ॥

Stanza 101: From the ascendant should be divined the nature (comfortable or otherwise) of the journey; from the 10th, the object; from the 7th the nature of the place to be visited; and from the 4th the result (or outcome) of the journey. From the Lagna should also be ascertained the bodily or physical comforts.

NOTES

There is also an interpretation that if the Muthasila between the 1st and 5th lords occurs in Lagna, the journey will be comfortable; in the 10th the object will be realised; in the 7th, the destination will be reached safely; and in the 4th, the object of the journey will be realised.

But the commentator simply says that from the house mentioned in stanza 101, the events assigned to them should be inquired into—*Lagna rasi vasath morgo sukha duhkhanubhave chintyam.*

दशमे शुभे च सिद्धिः कार्यस्यास्ते प्रयाति यत्स्थाने ।
तत्र शुभं च चतुर्थे परिणामः सुन्दरः कार्ये ॥ १०२ ॥

Stanza 102: Benefics in the 10th. confer success; in the 7th-good in the place of visit; and in the 4th—complete satisfaction of fulfilment

लग्नेशं शशिनं वा यः क्रूरस्तुदति तत्र मनुजर्क्षे ।
मनुजत्रिराशिके वा तदा भयं द्विपदतो गन्तुः ॥ १०३ ॥

जलराशौ वारिभयं चतुष्पदर्क्षे तथाऽश्वादेः ।
घटचापे दुमकंटकभयं हरौ व्याघ्रसिंहादेः ॥ १०४ ॥

Stanzas 103 and 104: According as the Lagna lord or the Moon is afflicted in human, quadruped or aquatic signs, the trouble during journey will come from human beings, four-legged animals or water resorting creatures respectively. If the affliction is in Sagittarius or Aquarius, the trouble will be from trees and plants. If the affliction is in Leo, the trouble will be from leonine species.

NOTES

Stanza 102 gives combinations for fulfilment of the object of journey.

A traveller (in ancient times) faced the risk of danger from thieves, robbers, stagnant pools, wild beasts, etc. Stanza 103 explains the nature of these troubles. The Lagna lord or the Moon is afflicted in some sign. If this happens to be a *Manuja* or *dwipada Rasi*, the traveller faces trouble from the attacks of robbers or unsocial elements. Dwipada Rasis are Gemini, Virgo and Libra. If the signs are watery ones—Cancer, Scorpio and Pisces—trouble will be from big fish, tortoises, crocodiles, etc., or pirates travelling on high seas, etc. If the affliction occurs in quadruped signs—Aries, Taurus—the trouble will be from quadrupeds—cattle, horses, sheep, etc. If the signs are Aquarius and Sagittarius, the traveller faces trouble from plants and trees. If the sign Leo is involved, wild beasts may attack him.

Even today considerable risks are involved in travel—accidents, robberies, etc., and these combinations have to be adapted to apply to modern conditions of travel. We are inclined to suggest, taking into account our own humble experience, that the nature of the signs—watery, fiery, earthy etc.—could be taken into consideration while applying these rules. Thus the lord of the ascendant in Gemini with Mars may indicate risk of accident while travelling in aeroplanes; if the sign, the lord of Lagna is in, is Aries with Mars situated therein, there is risk of the conveyance used catching fire, etc. There is much scope for research in this branch of horary astrology.

नगरप्रवेशतोऽस्मात् फलमस्ति न वा प्रवेशलग्नमिंह ।
तस्मिन्धनपे वक्रे नो हरणं कार्यसिद्धिर्वा ॥ १०५ ॥

Stanza 105: If the query "will my visit to the city or place prove beneficial" is put, it must be answered thus: If the lord of the 2nd is in the ascendant, retrograde, the querent's planned visit to the place will not be useful.

अतिचरिते बहुदिवसं हरणं नो कार्यसिद्धिरीषदपि ।
नवमतृतीयगतेऽस्मिन्कार्यम् कृत्वाऽऽशु निजपुरं याति ॥ १०६ ॥

Stanzas 106: If the second lord is in accelerated motion, the stay will not be long and the visit not much fruitful. If the second lord occupies the 9th or 3rd, the querent finishes his job quickly and returns back to his native place.

लग्ने कर्मण्याये धनपयुते शोभनं ज्ञेयम् ।
सक्रूरसप्तमस्थे पथि विघ्नाञ्झकटकश्चतुर्थस्थे ॥ १०७ ॥

Stanza 107: The lord of 2nd joining the ascendant, the 10th or 11th, indicates smooth fulfilment of the object of the visit. According as the 2nd lord is in the 7th or 4th, afflicted, the failure will be due to many troubles or quarrels on the way.

NOTES

For success or otherwise of the contemplated visit to a mofussil place, the main factor to be considered is the lord of the 2nd. His disposition denotes success or failure of the visit.

Summing up the various combinations we can say that the lord of the 2nd in the ascendant usually shows success of the object of a journey; in the 10th the querent will have success on the journey; a benefic in the 7th indicates he will have success in the place of his visit; in the 4th, success is indicated after his return home. In all these cases, the ascendant and the 2nd lord should be unafflicted.

The lord of the 9th in a movable sign shows quick journey and return home; if in a fixed sign long absence; and if in a common sign, change of route visiting other places etc. We can also guess whether the querent will fall ill or meet with mishaps by noting the affliction to the 2nd lord from the 6th or 8th lord. The final result or outcome rests on the disposition of the fourth house.

Tenth House Questions

राज्याप्तिप्रश्न लग्ने लग्नेशे शशिनि वा नभः पतिना ।
कृतमुथशिलेऽम्बदृशा राज्यं रूपक्रमाद्भवति ॥ १०८ ॥

Stanza 108: If the lord of the Lagna or the the Moon is in the ascendant forming Muthasila with the lord of the 10th and the 10th is aspected favourably, the querent inherits the kingdom he is heir to.

NOTES

Though this stanza ostensibly purports to answer a query pertaining to inheritance of kingdom, the combination can be applied to all matters pertaining to profession, office, trade, etc. The lord of the ascendant or the Moon must be in the Lagna in Muthasila with the lord of the 10th which should also receive a benefic aspect. The querent will secure a job, will inherit an estate, will get honour or will thrive well in his profession.

अन्योन्यभवनगमनात्क्रूराभावेऽथ चिन्तितत्राप्तिः ।
लग्नस्थे वाऽन्येन च सौम्येनाम्बरस्य सुथशिलेऽप्येवम् ।
पापर्दिते तु मन्दे निकटीभूयोत्तरत्यधो राज्यम् ॥ १०९ ॥

Stanza 109: The lords of the ascendant and the 10th in mutual interchange of houses and unafflicted confer gain (of kingdom) without effort. Lord of the 10th in the ascendant in Muthasila with a benefic indicates similar result. If in the above combination, the slower-moving planet is afflicted, the querent has no chance of success.

NOTES

According to stanza 109, one can gain office or preferment in his job under the following conditions:

(a) Lord of the ascendant should be in the 10th and vice versa, both unafflicted.

(b) Lord of the 10th in Muthasila with a benefic planet.

The result will be unfavourable if in the combination (b), of the planets in Muthasila, the one with slower velocity is afflicted either by conjunction with or aspect of malefics.

Suppose lord of the 10th is Mars and he is in Muthasila with Mercury. Mars is the slower-moving planet. If Mars is in conjunction with the Sun, Saturn or Rahu, then the benefic yoga is neutralised and the querent will get no preferment, promotion or acquisition.

भूमिस्थे क्रूरदृशा त्वपवादः शुभदृशा कीर्तिः ।
मन्दग्रहे बलवति, क्रूरवियुक्ते यदा शशी विबलः ॥ ११० ॥

मन्दे बलेन जमणात् राज्यप्राप्तिर्भवेत्प्रष्टुः ।
लग्नाधिपतौ स्वगृहे लाभे राज्यस्य तुंगगे भौमे ॥ १११ ॥

Stanzas 110 and 111: If a slow-moving planet is strongly placed in the 4th in adverse Muthasila (square aspect) the querent's reputation is in jeopardy; if in favourable Muthasila (trine) free from affliction, he gets fame. If the Moon is weak and the slow-moving planet is not devoid of strength, the querent gets the kingdom after visiting many places. If the ascendant lord is in the ascendant and Mars is exalted, the estate is secured.

NOTES

There is also another interpretation in a manuscript secured by me from a Pandit, *viz.*, if the 4th house is aspected by malefics, it affects the reputation; if by benefics, the querent gets fame. But this interpretation is not endorsed by Tajaka commentators.

Muthasila between a slower-moving planet strongly placed in the 4th and another in the 7th, ascendant or the 10th becomes adverse. Muthasila between the said planet in the 4th and another in the 8th and 11th is favourable.

लग्नाम्बराधिपौ यदि कंबूलौ केन्द्रगेन्दुमुथशिलतः ।
उत्तमराज्याचाप्तिः स्वर्क्षस्थे चेन्दुतो विपुला ॥ ११२ ॥

Stanza 112: When Kamboola Yoga is present due to the lords of the ascendant and the 10th being in Muthasila with a quadrangular Moon, the querent gets a good kingdom. If the Moon is situated in his own house, he gets an enlarged kingdom.

NOTES

When the lords of the Lagna and the significator (here the lord of the 10th) are in Muthasila and simultaneously the Moon has Muthasila with either of the two lords, Kamboola Yoga is formed. In the below given chart, lord of the ascendant is Mercury. The significator (lord of the 10th) is Jupiter. Mercury and Jupiter are in Muthasila (sextile). The Moon occupying a Kendra from Lagna has Muthasila with both the lords, involving them in Kamboola. The querent (as per the chart) should, according to Neelakanta, get a kingdom. In the modern context, he will secure preferment, position, etc., because of Kamboola Yoga.

Moon 12			Lagna
			Mercury 10
			Jupiter 14

On Realising the Object

यत्रर्क्षे लग्नेशस्तत्पतिरशुभे गृहे तदा कार्यम् ।
न स्यादस्ते कष्टाद्दशमदृशा कटुकता कार्ये ॥ ११३ ॥

Stanza 113: There will be no success or realisation of the object if the lord of the sign occupied by the lord of the ascendant is in unfavourable houses. Immense difficulties have to be faced if the ascendant lord is combust. If there is a square aspect, there will be strife and quarrels.

NOTES

This stanza deals with Karya Siddhi or success, and can be applied for answering questions bearing on general success or failure.

The unfavourable houses are the 6th, 8th and 12th (dusthanas). If the planet concerned (i.e., the ruler of the sign occupied by the ascendant lord) is in the 6th, 8th or 12th, and has a square aspect with another planet—here the planet must be in the 10th from the 6th, 8th or 12th—there will be no success; and quarrels will ensue.

In the chart below, the ascendant lord is in Pisces and the lord of this sign *viz.*, Jupiter is in the 12th from the ascendant. The Moon is in the 10th from Jupiter causing a square aspect. The query was about success or failure in regard to an interview the querent was about to seek for a good job. The answer given was "failure" and the person did not get the job.

Rahu 11 Saturn 28 Venus 7			Moon 26-53
	31-1-1969 at 11-50 p.m. (I.S.T.) at Bangalore		
Mercury 14 Sun 20			
		Mars 26 Lagna 11	Jupiter 14

Bhava Prasna

राज्यप्राप्तौ सत्यां यदि चेच्छति कोऽपि परिणतिं च तदा ।
लग्नं शरीरकार्यम् गृहकर्मास्तं नभश्च राज्यार्थम् ॥ ११४ ॥

लाभो मित्रस्यार्थे चतुर्थकं कर्मणोऽवसितये च
द्रव्यं धनाय सहजं भृत्येश्यो रिपुकृतेश्च वैरिभ्यः ॥ ११५ ॥

एतैः शुभैः शुभं स्यादशुभे वामं च सर्वकार्याणाम् ।
वित्तस्वामिनि भौमे नीचस्थे पारदारिके व्ययकृत् ॥ ११६ ॥

Stanzas 114 to 116: In a question "Is there any chance of my getting a kingdom", the Lagna represents physical efforts, the 7th signifies attempts at home, the 10th rules the advantages of securing the kingdom and the 4th comprehends the help derived from friends. The 2nd denotes financial help, the third, help from assistants and the 6th, the mind of the enemies. If these places are occupied by or conjoined with benefics, beneficial results flow from the respective significations. The reverse holds good if afflicted. If the lord of the 2nd being Mars is debilitated, money will be spent on others' wives.

NOTES

Winning a kingdom in ancient times meant help and opposition from a number of sources—one's own preparations, the advantages or otherwise of securing a kingdom. help from friends, financial advantages, help from one's own employees, attempts made by the enemy to thwart the aspirations of the querent, etc. Benefics in the appropriate houses facilitate the help from the sources signified by the appropriate houses. Afflictions indicate troubles and obstructions.

These combinations can be tried in answering questions bearing on securing of important positions, preferments, etc., where effort has to be put forth through different methods. The 2nd line of stanza 116 mentions expenditure of funds on other's wives if Mars is lord of the 2nd and is debilitated. It might be that others' wives were being bribed to help the querent in his attempts to secure a kingdom.

जीवे धर्मायरिपौ गुरुपूजायै सिते विलासाय ।
वाणिज्याय झे पुनरिन्दौ मुथशिलिनि चान्यथाऽन्यर्थम् ॥ ११७ ॥

Stanza 117: According as the lord of the 2nd is Jupiter, Venus or Mercury occupying the 9th, 11th or 6th, funds will be spent on helping preceptors, on sensual pleasures and on trade and business. If the Moon has Ithasala the motive in spending will be generous.

लग्नपतौ पतितस्थे विबले राज्यात्ययस्तु कम्बूले ।
कोपि गुण: स्यात्पापाक्रांतैरशुभं च्युतौ भवति ॥ ११८ ॥

Stanza 118: If the lord of Lagna is afflicted and weak, the kingdom will be destroyed. If Kamboola is present and the Yoga-producing planet is afflicted, the querent will fall from power.

NOTES

The stanzas are clear enough not needing any explanation.

नरपतिसचिवस्नेहप्रश्ने कम्बूललग्नसप्तमयो: ।
मुथशिलयो: शुभदृष्ट्या शुभता राज्ये मिथ: स्नेह: ॥ ११९ ॥

Stanza 119: Amity will exist between the king and the minister if there is Kamboola Yoga in the Lagna and the 7th and benefics are in Ithasala with the two houses.

NOTES

According to this stanza, the Lagna indicates the ruler-king, president or head of state and the 7th denotes the minister. If a question is put whether the ruler and the minister will have mutual understanding and amity, say they will be friendly if Kamboola Yoga exists in the chart involving the ascendant and the 7th house and benefics have Muthasila with these two places. I think the Kamboola and Muthasila should occur as between the lords and not the houses. When a planet causes Muthasila, say with the Lagna, there is bound to be a Muthasila with the 7th.

	Mars 22		
Moon 21			
		Lagna Venus 18	

Take the above chart. The ascendant (king) is Libra and the lord Venus is in 18° Libra. The lord of the 7th (minister) is in the 7th, Aries 22° and the Moon is in Aquarius 21. There is Ithasala between the lord of the ascendant and the seventh. Kamboola is present as the Moon is having Ithasala with both the lords. Hence the answer should be friendship exists between the ruler and his minister.

राज्यं चरं वा लग्नपगगनेशयो: सहयो: ।
यद्येको मन्द: स्यात्केन्द्र तत्स्थितमतोल वाच्यम् ॥ १२० ॥

यदि वा स वाममार्गे भूमौ वा प्रच्युतिर्भवेत् पूर्वम् ।
कम्बूले सति लभते शीघ्रन्त्वथ मुसरिफे न पुनः ॥ १२१ ॥

Stanzas 120 and 121: The query "whether or not the king holds the country permanently" should be answered thus: If out of the lords of the ascendant and the 10th, the slower-moving lord is in a quadrant, the authority will be permanent. Otherwise, the sway will be temporary.

If the slower-moving planet is retrograde and occupies the 4th house and there is Kamboola Yoga, the kingdom will slip out of the king's rule for some time but he gets it back quickly. If there is Musaripha, the chance of getting back the kingdom is bleak.

NOTES

Stanza 120 requires that out of the lords of the 1st and 10th, the slower moving should be in a quadrant to make the ruler's hold permanent. According to stanza 121, the kingdom will slip out of his hands and it will be restored to him again if the slower lord referred to in stanza 120, is in the 4th, retrograde, and there is Kamboola Yoga. If there is Musaripha, the loss is permanent.

Questions Pertaining to the Eleventh House

नृपतेगौरवलाभाशादि मम स्यान्न वेति च प्रश्ने ।
आयेशलग्नपत्योः स्नेहदृशामुथशिले दूतं भवति ॥ १२२ ॥

Stanza 122: If the question "will the king honour me" is put, answer it thus: If the lords of the 1st and 11th are in friendly Muthasila, the querent will be honoured.

रिपुदृष्ट्या बहुदिवसैः केन्द्रे चायेराचन्द्रकम्बूले ।
बाच्या पूर्णेवाशा चरस्थिरद्विःस्वभावगे स्वनामफलम् ॥ १२३ ॥

Stanza 123: If the aspect is unfriendly, the honour is delayed. If the lord of the 11th has a Kamboola Yoga with the Moon, in a Kendra, the honour will be conferred early. The result will be appropriate to the nature of the sign—movable, fixed or common to which the Kamboola has reference.

NOTES

Stanzas 122 and 123 can be used for predicting whether one will be successful in securing a desired object, or obtaining the friendship of others, etc., though the original slokas purport to predict—whether one will get a distinction or honour from the king.

When two planets are in conjunction or trine or opposition, sextile or square, the Ithasala or Muthasila Yogas are caused. The hostile aspect is square, conjuction and opposition. The favourable aspect is of course the trine. If there is an applying aspect, the faster-moving planet being behind the slower-moving planet, the result in the future will be favourable or unfavourable according to the nature of the aspect, Stanza 122 requires lords of the 11th and the ascendant to be in a trine aspect if the querent is to be honoured by the king. If the aspect is not friendly, then the honour is delayed. If the lord of the 11th has Kamboola Yoga with the Moon in a quadrant, then the honour is conferred. If the lord of the 11th has Kamboola Yoga with the Moon in a quadrant, honour will be conferred or the object in view will be fulfilled or the expected friendship realised or hoped—for the thing obtained. If the sign is movable, the honour granted or friendship acquired, etc. will not be lasting. If it is a fixed sign, the result is lasting and happy. A common sign shows a certain uncertainty regarding the nature or time of getting the honour.

In the illustration, given on next page lord of the ascendant Saturn is in 14° Taurus and lord of the 11th Mars in 12° Virgo. There is favourable Muthasila between the two lords. But the Moon has an Ithasala with the lord of the 11th Mars and the sign in which Mars is placed, is a movable one. Hence the honour secured may not last long.

		Saturn 14	
			Moon 8
Lagna			
			Mars 12

According to some commentators, the movable, fixed or common nature of the sign refers to the position of the lord of the 11th and not the Moon.

Aocording to this interpretation, the lord of the 11th is in a common or dual sign in the illustration The result is uncertainty. We feel the latter interpretation is more reasonable. We would like to split up the combination thus:

(a) There should be Kamboola between the Moon and the 11th lord.

(b) The 4th lord should be in a Kendra.

(c) The nature of this sign should be considered.

The following illustration will make the above three points clear.

		Lagna 6	Moon 5
Sun 9			
			Jupiter 12
Venus 14			

(a) The Moon has Kamboola with Jupiter lord of the 11th.

(b) This Sun is in a quadrant.

(c) Jupiter occupies a fixed sign. Hence the results are indicated by the nature of this sign.

It will be seen that Kamboola can occur only when there is Ithasala between the lord of Lagna and the significator, the Moon himself having Ithasala with either of these two lords.

मन्दे क्रूरोपहते भूत्वाऽऽशाऽऽशु प्रणाशमुपयाति ।
क्रूरायुक्ते च शुभयुज्यधिकारवशेन लब्ध्याशा ॥ १२४ ॥

Stanza 124: If the slower-moving planet is afflicted, the querent's hope will seem to be quickly fulfilled, but he will be actually disappointed. If the planet is not afflicted, the hope for honour will be confirmed.

NOTES

Of the two planets—the ascendant lord and the significator, that which has a slower velocity should be considered for applying the combination given in stanza 124.

मित्रेण सह प्रीतिर्भविता लग्नेश्वरायपत्योश्च ।
प्रियदृष्ट्या मुथशिलत: प्रीतिर्वाऽन्योन्बगृहयानात् ॥ १२५ ॥

Stanza 125: If the lords of the ascendant and the 11th are in mutual friendly Muthasila there will be real friendship between the querent and the quesited.

केन्द्रे स्थितयोरनयोमैत्री किल पूर्वजातैव ।
पणफरगतौ पुरस्तादापोक्लिमतो महाप्रीति ॥ १२६ ॥

Stanza 126: If the lords of the ascendant and the 11th are in mutual Kendras, there will be friendship; if in Panaparas there will be intimacy; and if in Apoklimas, bosom friendship will prevail.

NOTES

The Lagna indicates the querent and the lord of the 11th indicates the friends. If the question is asked "whether the person queried about will be friendly with me" say, he will be an intimate friend visiting the querent's house also if the lords of the ascendant

and the 11th are in favourable Muthasila, i.e., in 3rd, 5th, 8th or 11th from each other. Suppose, of the two lords, one (the Moon) is in Cancer 10° and the other (Venus) in Taurus 15°. Then there is friendly Muthasila and the querent and the quesited will be friends having intimate social contacts also visiting each other's house (अन्योन्यगृहयानात्). If the lords are in mutual Kendras or Panaparas, then also similar results will happen. If in Apoklimas, there will be great friendship.

Readers must carefully study the chapter—Ithasala Yogas—described in my book *Varshaphal* so that their understanding of this book becomes easy.

गुप्तं कार्यमिदं मे सिद्ध्यति लग्नेश्वरेऽथ चन्द्रमसि ।
शुभमथशिलगे केन्द्रे तन्निकटे वाऽथ सिद्धिः स्यात् ॥ १२७ ॥

Stanza 127: If the lord of Lagna and the Moon are in favourable Muthasila in a quadrant (Kendra) or in a cadent house (Panapara) the object of the querent will be fulfilled.

NOTES

The querent has an object or a plan which is secret (guptakarya). If the question "whether he will be successful or not in his secret plan" is put, then the answer is to be given on the basis of stanza 127. If the Muthasila has reference to an Apoklima house (3, 9, 12) then the plan or scheme will not succeed.

As we have said earlier, the combination, given in stanzas 122 to 127, can be used for answering questions bearing on realisation of objects, securing a hoped—for distinction or honour, and friendship.

According to our experience, lord of the ascendant in the 11th or vice versa, the Moon and lord of the 11th in mutually good aspects; lord of the 11th in an angle; or in a panapara involved in Kamboola Yoga—all indicate success. If the lord of the 11th favourably disposed as above is in a movable sign—expectation and disappointment; if in a fixed sign—complete success; and if in a common sign not much to be expected.

The querent will have sincere friendship if the lords of the ascendant and 11th are in good aspect with each other. Lord of the 12th in the 11th or hostile aspect to the lord of the 11th denotes a secret enemy under the guise of a friend.

Twelfth House Questions

रिपुविग्रहपृच्छायां बलवति षष्ठे रिपु: सबल: ।
द्वादशपे शुभदृष्टे बलवति वाच्यं बलं प्रष्टु: ॥ १२८ ॥

Stanza 128: In disputes with opponents, if the lord of the 6th is strong, the enemy should be considered as powerful. If the 12th lord is powerful, then the querent will be powerful.

रिपुविग्रहपृच्छायां नामोच्चारे रिपोर्बलिन्यस्ते ।
गुप्ते च द्वादशपे बलवति वाप्यं बलं प्रष्टु: ॥ १२९ ॥

Stanza 129: If the query is about war with an enemy, say the enemy is powerful if the lord of the 7th is strongly disposed. If the lord of the 12th is powerful, then the person for whom the query is put is more strongly placed.

NOTES

In horary astrology, the 6th should be taken to represent secret foes and the 7th should be taken to signify open enemies, such as contestants in elections, plaintiff or defendant in a civil case, the prosecutor in a criminal case, etc. The ascendant always signifies the querent. If the lord of the 7th is afflicted, it will have adverse effects on the opponent. If the lord of the 6th is afflicted, the secret foe (especially relatives) will suffer. If the lord of the ascendant is well placed and strong, the querent will succeed.

शुभयुतदृष्टे सद्ग्रचयमशुभेक्षणयोगतो व्ययमनर्थात् ।
एवं भावेष्वखिलेषूह्यां सदसत्फलं सुधिया ॥ १३० ॥

Stanza 130: If the 12th house is well aspected and conjoined, the querent will spend money on deserving causes. Otherwise the earnings will be squandered. In this way, each house should be studied.

NOTES

In the final analysis, whichever Bhava and its lord are strengthened, well aspected or conjoined, good results of the Bhava manifest. If the Bhava and the lord are afflicted, the events signified by the Bhava suffer.

Chapter 3

On Special Questions

Return of a Person in Exile

आगमने पृच्छायां लग्नेशे लग्नमध्यसंस्थेन ।
कृतसुशिले समेति हि सुखमस्ततुरीयगे कष्टात् ॥ १ ॥

Stanza 1: If the lord of the Lagna is in Muthasila with a planet in the Lagna or the 10th house, the traveller returns safely. If the lord of the ascendant is in the 7th or 4th or is in Muthasila with the lord of the 7th, he will return with much difficulty.

NOTES

The Lagna signifies the traveller or the missing person. The 7th rules the way, the 4th signifies the traveller's happiness. An Ithasala of the lord of the ascendant with a planet in the ascendant or the 10th favours safe return. The ascendant lord in the 4th or 7th or in Ithasala with the lord of the 7th signifies return with difficulty.

We would like to substitute the significator's house (e.g., 5th for son, 7th for wife or husband, etc.) for the traveller or absent person, the 7th there from for the way and the 4th there from for traveller's happiness.

According to *Tajakasara*, the missing person returns of his own accord if the lord of the 7th is in the ascendant.

स्थानाच्चलितः प्रश्ने लग्नपतौ सहजनवमगृहसंस्थे ।
लग्नस्थेन मुथशिले पन्थानं वहति पथिकोऽयम् ॥ २ ॥

Stanza 2: If the lord of Lagna occupies the 3rd or 9th and has Muthasila with a planet in the ascendant, the traveller is already on his way back.

NOTES

If the query is put whether a traveller or missing person is in the place to which he has gone or is suspected to have gone, then say he is already on his way back if the lord of Lagna occupying either the 3rd or 9th is in Muthasila with a planet in the ascendant, According to our experience, 5th house situation is also favoured.

रन्ध्रेऽस्थ धने तस्मिन्नाकाशस्थेन मुथ शिलेऽप्येवम् ।
केन्द्रस्थितेत्थशाले लग्नेक्षणवर्ज्यमेति न कदापि ॥ ३ ॥

Stanza 3: The ascendant lord occupying the 2nd or 8th house and in Ithasala with a planet in the 10th signifies that the traveller is on his way back. If the ascendant lord is in Muthasila with a planet in a quadrant and the Lagna is unaspected, the person will never return.

NOTES

For predicting the non-return of the missing person, lord of the ascendant should occupy the 2nd or the 8th and be in Muthasila with a planet in the 6th or 7th and the Lagna also should have no aspect on it. Muthasila with a planet in the 10th is favourable but not with a planet in the 4th or 7th.

लग्नाधिपतौ व लग्नं पश्यत्यमुत्र चन्द्रे वा ।
वक्रगमूथशिले सति समेति पथिक: सुखं शीघ्रम् ॥ ४ ॥

Stanza 4: If the lord of the ascendant is retrograde and the Moon is in the ascendant, in Muthasila with a retrograde planet, the person will soon return safely.

अन्त्यस्थितलग्नपतौ शशिना कृतमुथशिले द्रुतमुपैति ।
लग्नद्वाऽपि चतुर्थाच्छुभाद् द्वितीयतृतीयगा वाऽपि ॥ ५ ॥

Stanza 5: The traveller will return early if the Moon is in Muthasila with the lord of Lagna occupying the 12th. If benefic planets, are in the 2nd or 3rd from Lagna or from the 4th or the signs held by benefic planets, traveller returns soon.

NOTES

The return of the missing person or fugitive will happen soon when:

(a) The lord of Lagna be retrograde, the Moon is in Lagna having Ithasala with another planet in retrogression.

(b) The lord of the Lagna occupying the 12th is in Muthasila with the Moon.

(c) Benefics occupy the 2nd or 3rd from the ascendant, from the fourth or from other benefic planets in the Prasna chart.

Combination (c) can also be applied for predicting recovery of lost property.

The following is quoted by the author from *Prasna Chinthamani.*

Missing Person: Alive or Dead?

ग्रहः षष्ठेऽथ जामित्रे वापपतिः कंटके स्थितः ।
पथिकागमनं ब्रूते सिते ज्ञे वा त्रिकोणगे ॥ ६ ॥

Stanza 6: The missing person will return if any planet occupies the 6th or 7th, Jupiter is in a quadrant and Mercury and Venus are in trines.

पुष्णोदये पापदृष्टे शुभदृग्वर्जिते बुधः ।
लग्नात्षष्ठे यदा पापा यातुश्च निधनं वदेत् ॥ ७ ॥

Stanza 7: The traveller should be deemed to have been dead if the ascendant is a Prushtodaya sign aspected by malefics and devoid of benefic aspects and the 6th house is occupied by Mercury afflicted by malefics.

यदा क्रूरास्तृतीयस्था देशाद्देशान्तरं गतः ।
चौरेणैव हृतस्वश्च पथिकः केन्द्रगा यदि ॥ ८ ॥

Stanza 8: The person will have gone from one place to another if malefics occupy the third. His money will have been robbed if malefics are in quadrants.

पापैः षष्ठत्रिलाभस्थैः कंटकस्थैः शुभग्रहैः ।
प्रवासी सुखमायाति दूरस्थोऽपि सुनिश्चितम् ॥ ९ ॥

Stanza 9: If malefics are in the 3rd, 6th and 11th and benefics in quadrants, the missing person, no matter how far he may be, will return safe.

चतुरस्रे त्रिकोणे वा पापगेहस्थितः शनिः ।
पापदृष्टश्च नियतं बन्धनं यातुरादिशेत् ॥ १० ॥

Stanza 10: The traveller will be in custody if Saturn occupies a malefic sign identical with a quadrant or a trine and is aspected by malefics.

शुभयुक्ते स्थिरे लग्ने स्थिरो बन्धश्चरेऽन्यथा ।
द्वितनौ सौम्यसंयुक्ते बन्धमोक्षो क्रमेण तु ॥ ११ ॥

Stanza 11: The traveller will be held in custody permanently, or for some time arrested and released according as the ascendant occupied by benefics, is a fixed, movable or common sign.

पापस्त्रिकोणजामित्रे विलग्ने पृष्ठकोदये ।
शत्रुभिर्वीक्ष्यमाणाश्च यातुः कष्टं वदेन्सुधीः ॥ १२ ॥

Stanza 12: If malefics occupy the 7th or the trines and the ascendant being a Prushtodaya sign is aspected by malefics, the traveller will be subjected to many troubles and difficulties.

मार्गस्थानगतैः सौम्यैर्भांगं तस्य शुभं भवेत् ।
क्रूरैर्दुःखं विलग्नस्थैः पापैः क्लेशमवाप्नुयात् ॥ १३ ॥

Stanza 13: Benefic planets in the 7th indicate the safety of the traveller. Malefics in the ascendant, denote difficulties for him.

चरलग्ने चरांशे वा चतुर्थे चन्द्रमाः स्थितः ।
प्रवासी सुखमायाति कृतकार्यश्च वेश्मनि ॥ १४ ॥

Stanza 14: If the Lagna of the Navamsa Lagna is a movable sign and the Moon occupies the 4th, the person will return home safely after completing his work.

कंटकैः सौम्यसंयुक्तैः पापग्रहविवर्जितः ।
प्रवासी सुखमायाति तिधनस्थे सुधाकरे ॥ १५ ॥

Stanza 15: If the quadrants are occupied by benefics and unafflicted by malefics or if the Moon is in the 8th, the traveller will be back home safe.

गमागमौ तु न स्यातां योगे दुरुधुराकृते ।
शुभैःशुभकृतो रोघः पापैस्तस्करतो भयम् ॥ १६ ॥

Stanza 16: If Durdhura Yoga is present, the traveller will be where he is. If benefics cause Durdhura, it forebodes good for the traveller. If malefics cause the Yoga, he will suffer because of enemies and thieves.

NOTES

Stanzas 6 to 16 do not need any explanation because they are clear. Durdhura Yoga, referred to in stanza 16, is caused when the Moon has planets on either side. The Durdhura is benefic or malefic according as the planets situated on either side of the Moon are benefics or malefics.

गमागमौ हि न स्यातां स्थिरराशौ बिलग्ने ।
न रोगोपशमो नाशो द्रव्याणां च पराभवः ॥ १७ ॥

Stanza 17: If the Lagna is a fixed sign, then the traveller will remain where he is; the illness will not be cured; lost money will not be recovered; failure will be the result.

NOTES

The first line of the stanza is relevant to the subject in view, *viz.*, the whereabouts of the traveller. If a question concerns illness, theft or victory and the same combination is present, the result will be unfavourable.

विपरीतं चरे वाच्यं फलं मिश्र द्विमूर्तिषु ।
स्थिरवत्प्रथमे खण्डे परार्धे चरराशिवत् ॥ १८ ॥

Stanza 18: If the Lagna is Chara, contrary results happen. If the Lagna is a common sign, the first and second halves denote results similar to fixed and movable signs respectively.

NOTES

If the ascendant is a movable sign (Chara Rasi), the missing person will return, lost article is recovered, the sick person recovers and victory attends the querent. If the 1st part of a common sign rises, the results will be similar to those signified by a fixed sign. If the second half of a common sign is the Lagna, the results will be similar to those signified by a Chara Lagna.

प्रवासी शीघ्रमायाति गुरुशुक्रौ त्रिवित्तगौ ।
चतुर्थस्थानगावेतौ शीघ्रमायाति कार्यकृत् ॥ १९ ॥

Stanza 19: The traveller will get back soon if Jupiter and Venus are in the 3rd or 2nd house. If they are in the 4th, he will return home soon after completing his mission.

इन्दुः सप्तमगो लग्नात् पथिकं वक्ति मार्गगम् ।
मार्गाधिपश्च राश्यर्धात्परभागे व्यवस्थितः ॥ २० ॥

Stanza 20: If the Moon is in the 7th house or if the lord of the 7th is in the second Hora of a sign, the traveller will be on his way back home.

NOTES

The disposition of Jupiter and Venus in the 2nd, 3rd or 4th is favourable for the speedy return of the missing person. He will be on his return journey if the Moon is in the 7th or the lord of the 7th is in the latter half of a sign. Second Hora means latte half of sign.

On Special Questions

शुक्रार्कजीवसौम्यानामेकोऽपि स्याद्धरायगः ।
तदाऽऽशु गमनं ब्रूयात्प्रष्टुनं गमनं व्यये ॥ २१ ॥

Stanza 21: If Venus, the Sun, Jupiter or Mercury is in the 4th or 11th, then return of the missing person should be expected soon. If any one of these planets is in the 12th, the person will not return.

NOTES

Venus or the Sun or Jupiter or Mercury should be in the 4th or 11th for the return; and in the 12th for non-return.

लग्नाद्यावथिथे स्थाने वली खेटो व्यवस्थितः ।
ब्रूयात्तावतिथे मासे पथिकस्य निवर्तनम् ॥ २२ ॥

Stanza 22: The fugitive will return from the foreign country in as many months as the number of signs intervening between the Lagna and the strongest planet.

NOTES

Suppose in a Prasna chart which indicates the return of a traveller the Lagna is Sagittarius and the strongest planet happens to be the Moon situated in Cancer. The intervening number of signs from the ascendant to Cancer is seven. Therefore, the fugitive may return in seven months' time.

एवं कालं यरांशस्थे द्विगुणं च स्थरांशके ।
द्विस्वभावांशगे खेटे त्रिगुणं चिन्तयेत्सुधीः ॥ २३॥

Stanza 23: The above period of return is for movable signs. According as the strongest planet is in a fixed or a common sign, the number is to be doubled or trebled.

NOTES

Suppose the number of signs intervening between the ascendant and the strongest planet is 6 and the planet is in a fixed sign. Then the time of return will be 12 months. If the planet considered is in a common sign, the period of return will be 18 months.

यातुर्विलग्नाज्जामित्रभवनाधिपतिर्यदा ।
करोति वक्रमावृत्ते: कालं तु ब्रुवते परे ॥ २४ ॥

Stanza 24: The time of return may also coincide with the time of the lord of the 7th becoming retrograde.

NOTES

Suppose lord of the 7th is Mars and he begins to retrograde, say after about 30 days from the date of question. The missing person will return in 30 days' time, provided the lord of the 7th is in a moveable sign. The period is to be doubled or trebled according as the lord of the 7th is posited in a fixed or common sign.

चतुर्थे दशमे वाऽपि यदि सौम्यग्रहो भवेत् ।
तदा न गमनं क्रूरैस्तत्रस्थैर्गमनं भवेत् ॥ २५ ॥

Stanza 25: If benefic planets occupy the 4th and 10th, the traveller will not return. Malefics in the above places indicate the return of the person.

लग्नाद्वा लग्ननाथाद्वा यत्संख्या: क्रूरखेचरा: ।
नवमे द्वादशे वाऽपि तत्संख्या: स्युरुपद्रवा: ॥ २६ ॥

Stanza 26: The person will meet with as many difficulties as the number of malefics that are situated in the 9th or 12th from Lagna or the Lagna lord.

लग्नाद्वा लग्ननाथाद्वा यावंत: सौम्यखेचरा: ।
मार्गे तत्रोदया वाच्या: स्थाने स्थाने विचशणै ॥ २७ ॥

Stanza 27: The traveller will meet with as many benefits on the way as the number of benefic planets that are occupying the 9th or 12th from the Lagna or Lagna lord.

NOTES

This combination is so worded that it is not possible to apply it unless inferential ability helps the astrologer. Supposing the 9th place from the ascendant lord has three malefics or three benefics. Then the traveller has to encounter three difficulties or three benefits on the way. What is the nature of the difficulty or the benefit and how it is to be inferred in the light of present-day conditions are matters which the astrologer has to decide by himself.

क्रूरयुक्तक्षितो मन्द: शुभदृग्योगवर्जित: ।
धर्मस्थस्तनुते व्याधि प्रोषितस्याष्टगो मृतिम् ॥ २८ ॥

Stanza 28: According as afflicted Saturn devoid of beneficial aspects is in the 9th or 8th, the traveller suffers from illness, or dies in a foreign place.

NOTES

Here affliction means association with malefics or being aspected by them. If Saturn is with Mars or the Sun and not having the aspect or association of Venus or Jupiter, he is considerably afflicted. When he is in the 9th, the traveller suffers sickness. When he is in the 8th, the traveller. will die in the place he has gone to.

जामित्रस्य शुमोत्थे याता नायाति दुरुधुरायोगे ।
मित्रस्वामिनिषेधात्पापोत्थे शत्रुरुक्चौरात् ॥ २९ ॥

Stanza 29: The traveller will be prevented from returning either by friends, or by enemies, illness or thieves according as the Moon's Durdhura Yoga in the 7th is caused by benefics or malefics.

NOTES

If the Moon is situated in the 7th, with a benefic each in the 6th and 8th, there is Subha Durdhura Yoga. In such a case, due to friendly pressure, etc., the traveller may not return. If, on the other hand, the Moon is in the 7th and malefics are in the 6th and 8th, causing Papadurdhura, the person will not be able to return because of the trouble from foes, thieves or ill-health.

चन्द्रार्कयोश्छिद्रगयोर्यमेन संदृष्टयोः स्यात्परशस्त्रभीतिः ।
रन्ध्रे सिते ज्ञे च सुखाप्तिरारे मन्दे भयं पापयुगीक्षितेऽध्वनि ॥ ३० ॥

Stanza 30: If the Sun and the Moon are in the 6th aspected by Saturn, the traveller will have fear from enemy's weapons. If Mercury or Venus is in the 11th, he will be happy. If Mars or Saturn is in the 8th, afflicted, he will encounter troubles on the way.

NOTES

Stanza 10 to 30 are from *Prasna Chintamani*.

Whether the Traveller is Alive or Dead

लग्नेश्वरे शीतकरेऽथ षष्ठे तुर्येऽष्टमे वाऽप्यतिनीचगे वा ।
अस्तंगते छिद्रपतीत्थशालयुक्तं शुभैर्दूरगतो मृतः स्यात् ॥ ३१ ॥

Stanza 31: If the lord of Lagna or the Moon is in the 6th, 4th or 8th, debilitated or combust, has Ithasala with the lord of the 8th and benefics are away, the traveller should be presumed to be dead.

NOTES

In the above combinations benefics should not conjoin with or aspect the ascendant or the Moon occupying the 6th, 4th or 8th, etc. Ithasala with the lord of the 8th indicates death of the person gone to a foreign land, missing person, etc.

भूमेरधःस्थेन च वक्रगेण यदीत्थशालं कुरुते शशांकः ।
सौम्यैरदृष्टे मरणं प्रकुर्यादूरस्थितस्यापि विदेशगस्य ॥ ३२ ॥

Stanza 32: The person gone to a distant dead if the place should be considered as Moon is in Ithasala with a retrograde planet occupying the 1st, 2nd or 3rd house which should be devoid of benefics.

सौम्यै: षष्ठान्त्यरन्ध्रस्तैविबलैश्च शुभेक्षितै: ।
पापयुक्तौ शशाङ्काको तदा दूरस्थितो मृत: ॥ ३३ ॥

Stanza 33: If benefics are in the 6th, 8th or 12th devoid of strength and aspected by malefics; or if the Sun and the Moon are affflicted by malefics, the person is dead.

पृष्ठोदये पापयुते त्रिकोणकेन्द्राष्टषष्ठोपगतश्च पापै: ।
सौम्यै रदृष्ट: परदेशसंस्थो मृतो गदार्तो नवमे च सूर्ये ॥ ३४ ॥

Stanza 34: The ascendant being a Prishtodaya sign occupied by malefics, malefic planets occupy trines, quadrants or the 8th or the 6th unaspected by benefics, the traveller is dead. If the Sun is in the 9th, he is suffering from illness.

तुर्योपरिस्थेन खगेन चन्द्रमा यदीत्थशालं कुरुते शुभेक्षितः ।
सौम्यैर्युतो वा परदेशसंस्थितः सुखी च जीवेत्पथि
सौख्यमेति ॥ ३५ ॥

Stanza 35: When the Moon has Ithasala with a planet placed in a house beyond the 4th, and is aspected by or conjoined with benefics, the traveller who has gone abroad is happy and returns safely.

According to the commentator, the planet with whom the Moon is to enter Ithasaia should occupy the 5th, 6th, 7th, 8th, 9th or 10th and should be free from affliction. This assures the well-being of the traveller in the far-off place he may be in and his subsequent safe return.

मार्गान्निवर्तते शत्रुः पापैः शत्रुगृहाश्रितैः ।
चतुर्थगैरपि प्राप्तः शत्रुर्भग्नो निवर्तते ॥ ३६ ॥

Stanza 36: If malefics are in inimical signs, the enemy will beat a retreat in the middle of the journey. If they are in the 4th, the enemy's retreat will follow with defeat.

झषालिकुम्भककर्कटा रसातले यदा स्थिताः ।
रिपोः पराजयस्तदा चतुष्पदैःपलायनम् ॥ ३७ ॥

Stanza 37: When the fourth house is identical with Pisces, Scorpio, Aquarius or Cancer, the enemy will suffer defeat: if it falls in a quadruped sign, the enemy will retreat.

मेषधनुसिंहवृषा यद्युदयस्था भवन्ति हिबुके वा ।
शत्रुनिवर्ततेऽत्र ग्रहसहिता वा वियुक्ता वा ॥ ३८ ॥

Stanza 38: The enemy will beat a retreat if the Lagna or the 4th house falls in Aries, Leo, Sagittarius or Taurus, whether or not such house is occupied by any planets.

नागच्छति परचक्रं यदाऽर्कचन्द्रौ चतुर्थभवनस्थो ।
गुरुबुधशुक्रा हिबुके यदा तदा शीघ्रमायाति ॥ ३९ ॥

Stanza 39: The enemy will not arrive if the 4th is occupied by the Sun and the Moon. Jupiter, Venus and Mercury in the 4th denote early invasion by the enemy.

स्थिरोदये जीवशनैश्चरे स्थिते गमागमौ नैव वदेत्तु पृच्छतः ।
त्रिपञ्चषष्ठा रिपुसंगमाय पापाश्चतुर्था निनिवर्तनाय ॥ ४० ॥

Stanza 40: If Saturn or Jupiter occupies Lagna, which should be a fixed sign, no forecast should be given to the querent. Malefics in the 3rd, 5th and 6th denote conflict with the enemy. He (the enemy) will be defeated if malefics are in the 4th.

दशमोदयसप्तमगाः सौम्या नगराधिपस्य विजयकराः ।
आराकौं झगुरुसिताः प्रभंगदौ विजयदा नवमे ॥ ४१ ॥

Stanza 41: The ruler will win if benefics occupy the 10th, 1st or 7th. Mars and Saturn in the 9th cause defeat to the querent—king. Mercury, Jupiter and Venus in the 9th denote victory.

उदयक्षर्याच्चन्द्रक्षं भवति च यावद्दिनैश्च तावद्धिः ।
आगमनं स्याच्छत्रोर्यदि न हि मध्ये ग्रहः कश्चित् ॥ ४२ ॥

Stanza 42: The enemy's invasion may happen within as many days as are signified by the number of signs intervening between the ascendant and the Moon, provided there are no planets in between.

NOTES

Stanzas 36 to 42 have been reproduced by Neelakantha from Prithuyasu's *Shatpanchasikha*, a rare work on Horary Astrology. They are intended to predict victory in war, defeat of the enemy or his retreat, etc. According to stanza 36, the enemy will run away after being defeated on the battle-field if malefics are in the 4th. The first line of the stanza given in certain editions of *Shatpanchasikha* reads : सुत शत्रुगतैः पापैः शत्रुमार्गानिवर्तते। Malefics in the 5th and 6th indicate the enemy will return on the way to attack and not as given in Prasna Tantra. However, Neelakantha's version is to be preferred. Stanza 37 says that if the 4th house falls in Pisces, Scorpio or Aquarius or Cancer, the enemy is vanquished. He is beaten and then he takes to heels if a quadrupedal sign is in the 4th. Quadrupedal signs are Taurus, Aries, Leo and Sagittarius. The words *Chatishpadathi palayanam* is translated by some authors as "retreat with quadrupeds". Neelakantha's commentator clearly says *satroh palayanam bhavet*, *i.e.*, the enemy retreats if the 4th house is a quadrupedal sign— *chatursthane chatushpada rasi gataihi*.

Even without being occupied by planets, defeat stares the enemy if in the Prasna chart Lagna or the 4th house falls in Aries, Leo, Taurus or Sagittarius. Obviously this stanza (No. 38) appears to be a repetition of the latter half of the previous one, except that the word "Lagna" is added.

Benefics in the 4th are not recommended as it indicates enemy's aggression. On the contrary, the Sun or the Moon in the 4th favours the victim of aggression (Stanza 39).

Stanza 40 warns us that no prediction, good or bad, should be given in case a fixed sign rises occupied by Jupiter or Saturn. But when malefics are in the 3rd, 5th and 6th, conflict with the enemy is shown. In the first part of the stanza, the reference is to the situation of Jupiter and Saturn. The word *veekshita* (aspect) is used in another version of *Shatpancha sikha*.

Stanza 41 is clear and needs no explanation.

Regarding the time factor as to when a threatened aggression can happen, stanza 42 indicates a principle which, it occurs to us, does not work, at least in modern times. If suppose the ascendant at the time of the query is Aries and the Moon is in Scorpio, then the number of signs intervening in between these two factors is 8. And the invasion may take place within 8 days. If there is a planet in between the ascendant and the Moon, then this principle cannot be applied.

Many of these combinations were framed at a time when mutual aggressions between petty chiefs were the order of the day. But we can adapt them to suit modern conditions only after considerable research.

दैत्येज्यवाचस्पतिसोमपुत्रैरेकक्ष्र्गैर्लग्नतैर्बलाढयै: 1
द्वाभ्यामथेज्ये भृगजेऽथ लग्ने हन्याद्रणे यायिनृपं पुरेश: ॥ ४३ ॥

Stanza 43: If strong Venus, Jupiter and Mercury or if at least two of these, or if Jupiter or Venus be in Lagna, the enemy ruler will be killed in the battlefield.

NOTES

This and the following six stanzas are from *Prasna Pradeepa*. According to the commentator, Venus,

Jupiter and Mercury should occupy one sign or at least two of them or them or Jupiter or Venus should be in the ascendant.

सूर्येन्दुभौमार्कजसैहिकेयैः सर्वेश्चतुभिस्त्रिभिरेव लग्नगैः ।
हन्यात्तदा स्थायिनमाशु यायी द्यूनस्थितैर्यायिनृप पुरेशः ॥ ४४ ॥

Stanza 44: If the Sun, the Moon, Mars, Saturn and Rahu or four of them or at least three of them occupy the Lagna, the querent king will meet with quick death. If these planets are in the 7th, the enemy king will meet with immediate death.

NOTES

Obviously the ascendant rules the querent or his agent and the 7th rules the enemy.

शुक्रेज्यशीतांशुबुधामरेज्यैः सर्वैस्त्रिभिर्द्यूनमतेर्बलाढ्यैः ।
हन्याद्रणे स्थायिनमाशु यायो सुखास्पदस्थैश्च
शुभैः सुसन्धिः ॥ ४५ ॥

Stanza 45: If Venus, Jupiter, the Moon and Mercury, or at least three of them in strength, occupy the 7th house, the enemy will quickly inflict defeat on the querent king. If benefics are in the 4th and 10th, the parties will sign a treaty.

कुजेत्थशाले हिमगौ विलग्ने बन्धोऽथ मृत्युर्युधि नागरस्य ।
भौमेत्थशाले च विधौ कलत्रे बन्धं मृतिं वा
लभतेऽत्र यायी ॥ ४६ ॥

Stanza 46: If the Moon occupying Lagna has Ithasala with Mars, the querent will be captured or killed. A similar fate befalls the enemy if the Moon (having Ithasala with Mars) occupies the 7th.

लग्नेशजामित्रपयोश्च मध्ये भवेद्ग्रहो यः स्वगृहोच्चसंस्थः ।
तद्वर्गमत्या नृपयोश्च संधिर्ज्ञेयो बुधैर्लेखकपण्डिताभ्याम् ॥ ४७ ॥

Stanza 47: Peace between the parties will be brought about by the person signified by planets in exaltation or own house, who are situated in between the lords of the ascendant and the 7th. If such a planet is Mercury, the mediator will be a writer or a scholar.

NOTES

Stanza 45 is clear. According to stanza 46, the Moon must be in Lagna or the 7th having Ithasala to denote the capture and death of the querent or the enemy respectively.

According to stanza 47, find out if any planets are exalted or in own house, between signs occupied by the lords of the ascendant and the 7th. If such a planet is the Sun or the Moon, the parties will agree to end the war with the consent of the sovereign; if Mars—commander-in-chief; if Mercury—by learned men or writers; if Jupiter or Venus,—preceptors, priests and ministers; and if Saturn—by subordinates.

क्रूरे कलत्रे ह्रदये शुभग्रहो यच्छेद्धनं यायिनृपाय नागरः ।
विपर्ययाद्यायिनृपः पुरेश्वरं रुर्गाद्विनिष्काश्य
                                   ददाति वास्पदम् ॥ ४८ ॥

Stanza 48: If malefics are in the 7th and benefics in the ascendant, the enemy is paid a ransom. If *vice-versa* the enemy pays ransom to the querent-ruler.

रवीत्थशाले शशिजे सुगुप्ताश्चरा भवेयुश्च कुजेसराफात् ।
ग्रहाच्छशाङ्केन युतश्च तस्मिन् ये ऽन्यवेषाश्च
                                   भवन्ति चाराः ॥ ४९ ॥

Stanza 49: If Mercury occupies the 7th and has Ithasala with the Sun, the spies will be in incognito. If Mars is in Easarpha with the Moon, the spies will don the dress signified by the planet in association with the Moon.

NOTES

The defendant or the enemy will come to an understanding by receiving or paying a ransom or bribe according to the situation of malefics in the 7th or the 1st house.

The enemy's spies will be incognito if Mercury occupying the 7th has Ithasala with the Sun. Mars can have Easarpha when the Moon has an Ithasala with him and also with another planet. The other planet in conjunction with the Moon denotes the way the spies dress. If the planet is Saturn, they will dress like servants. If the planet is Mercury they may dress like learned men, etc.

Attacking The Fortress

The following are from *Prasna Chinthamani*.

प्रश्ने विलग्ने क्रूरे वा दुर्गंभङ्गो हि जायते ।
विशेषतो भूमिपुत्रे राहौ वा मूर्तिगे सति ॥ ५० ॥

Stanza 50: The fortress will be taken if malefics are in Lagna at the time of query. This will be specially so if the malefic happens to be Mars or Rahu.

NOTES

Here the fort referred to represents the defences of the ruler that is attacked. The enemy will be able to breach the defences of the ruler who has been attacked if a malefic is in the ascendant. If Rahu or Mars happens to be such a malefic, the fortress of the defender will easily fall.

सप्तमे सिंहिकासूनो दुर्गं शीघ्रेण लभ्यते ।
जामित्रोदयगे क्रूरे रि:फगे लग्ननायके ॥ ५१ ॥

द्वितीये वाऽष्टमें षष्ठे तदा दुर्गं न लभ्यते ।
सक्रूरो लग्रपो वक्री युद्धद: केन्द्रसंस्थित: ॥ ५२ ॥

Stanzas 51 and 52: The fortress will be secured quickly when Rahu is in the 7th. If malefics are in Lagna or the 7th and the lord of Lagna is in the 12th, 2nd, 8th or 6th the fortress cannot be taken back again. If the ascendant lord associated with malefics is retrograde and occupies a Kendra, war is inevitable.

NOTES

The ascendant represents the querent or his party The 7th signifies the enemy, the invader or adversary. The affliction of the ascendant and its lord betokens suffering and defeat. The affliction of the 7th and its lord denotes defeat, etc., for the adversary.

षष्ठाधिपे धूनगते पापे वा युद्धमादिशेत् ।
पृच्छायां केन्द्रगै: क्रूरै: कीटे दुर्गे वधो नृणाम् ॥ ५३ ॥

Stanza 53: Lord of the 6th or malefics in the 7th denotes war. Malefics occupying quadrants, and especially Scorpio or Cancer, indicates the destruction of the fortress.

भौमाष्टमेशावेकत्र तदाऽतिनिधनं नृणाम् ।
स्वायपुत्रस्थिते जीवे कीटमध्ये भयं नहि ।
शनौ भौमे च केन्द्रस्थे बहूनां वधबन्धनम् ॥ ५४ ॥

Stanza 54: Mars and lord of the 8th in conjunction forebodes colossal slaughter.

Jupiter in the 2nd, 5th or 11th, which should be a Keeta Rasi, indicates no such destruction. If Saturn and Mars are in quadrants, there will be heavy destruction and capture of troops by the enemy.

NOTES

The above stanzas give combinations for declaration of war, destruction of defences and capture of prisoners. Obviously these results happen with reference to the querent or his party.

लग्नगतो यदि पाप: पापेन युतेक्षितो वा स्यात् ।
लग्नात्पूर्वापरगौ पापौ युद्धं तदा घोरम् ॥ ५५ ॥

Stanza 55: A war of great destruction will be declared if malefics are in or aspect the Lagna or the Lagna is hemmed in between malefics.

On the Recovery of the Patient, Etc.

विलग्ने षष्ठप: पापो जन्मराशिं निरीक्षते ।
रोगिणस्तस्य मरणं निश्चयेन वदेद्बुध: ॥ ५६ ॥

Stanza 56: The patient's death is certain when the ascendant is occupied by the lord of the 6th and the Moon is aspected by malefics.

NOTES

According to another version, if lord of the 6th or malefics occupying Lagna aspect the Moon, the patient queried about will die.

On Special Questions

चतुर्थाष्टमगे चन्द्रे पापमध्यगतेऽपि वा ।
मृतिः स्याद्बलसंयुक्तसौम्यदृष्ट्याऽचिरात्सुखम् ॥ ५७ ॥

Stanza 57: The Moon in the 4th or 8th house hemmed in between malefics denotes the death of the patient. The patient will recover early if the Moon is strongly placed and aspected by benefics.

विधौ लग्ने स्मरे भानौ रोगी याति यमालयम् ।
प्रश्ने क्रूरग्रहे लग्ने रोगवृद्धिश्चिकित्सकात् ॥ ५८ ॥

Stanza 58: The sick person will depart to the abode of Yama if the Moon is in the ascendant and the Sun is in the 7th. The disease or illness will become complicated by the physician's treatment when malefics are in the ascendant.

NOTES

The Moon's affliction especially in the 8th is not a sign for recovery. Papakarthari Yoga, i.e., malefics occupying either side of the Moon is always productive of harmful results. If both the lord of the ascendant and the Moon are in the 8th, afflicted, the patient's recovery is very doubtful.

According to stanza 58, if a question about the recovery of a sick man is put at sunset on a full Moon day, one has to predict death.

Doctors will complicate the disease if malefics are in the ascendant. In the modern times, innumerable instances could be cited of wrong diagnosis of diseases, rendering the patient more miserable. And perhaps in ancient times also no two doctors agreed.

तथा लग्नगते सौम्ये वैद्योक्तममृत वच: ।
लग्नं वैद्यो द्युनं व्याधि: खं रोगी तुर्यमौषधम् ॥ ५९ ॥

Stanza 59: If benefics are in the ascendant, the diagnosis will be correct. The Lagna signifies the physician, the 7th represents the nature of the disease or sickness, the 10th rules the sick person and the 4th denotes treatment.

NOTES

Stanza 59 gives interesting details allocating house-rulerships to the physician, the patient, illness and treatment. Depending upon the house afflicted, one can guess the result pertaining to the house. If the Lagna is well disposed, the doctor hits at correct diagnosis. If it is afflicted, he may bungle. The disease will be of a complicated nature if the 7th house is afflicted. If the 4th is afflicted, wrong medicines will be administered. According to another version, the 6th signifies the nature of disease.

This part of horary astrology can be of great importance to medical men in the treatment of their patients and to take proper care in diagnosing and administering medicines.

रोगिणो भिषजो मैत्री मैत्री भेषजरोगयो: ।
व्याधेरुपशमो वाच्य: प्रकोप: शात्रवे तयो: ॥ ६० ॥

Stanza 60: If there is friendship between the lords of the 1st and 10th houses, the treatment being appropriate to the disease, the illness will be cured. Otherwise, the disease aggravates.

NOTES

The treatment prescribed by the physician will be correct and recovery assured if the lords of the 1st and 10th are friends. If they are mutual enemies, complications will set in because of administering medicines not appropriate to the disease.

लग्ननाथे च सबले केन्द्रसंस्थे शुभग्रहे ।
उच्चगे वा त्रिकोणे वा रोगी जीवति निश्चयम् ॥ ६१ ॥

Stanza 61: The sick man is sure to survive, if the ascendant lord being a benefic is strongly disposed in a quadrant, is exalted or occupies Moolatrikona.

NOTES

The lord of the Lagna being a benefic should be strongly placed in a Kendra, or exalted or occupy a Moolatrikona place. The Moolatrikonas for the Sun, Moon, Mars, Mercury, Jupiter, Venus and Saturn respectively are Leo, Taurus, Aries, Virgo, Sagittarius, Libra and Aquarius.

This stanza is also interpreted by some commentators thus: "Lord of the ascendant strong and benefics occupying Moolatrikona or exaltation place which should be Kendras".

एकः शुभो बली लग्ने त्रायते रोगपीडितम् ।
सौम्या धर्मारिलाभस्थास्तृतीयस्था गदापहाः ॥ ६२ ॥

Stanza 62: A single planet, which should be powerful and a benefic occupying the Lagna, protects the sick man. If benefics are in the 9th, 6th, 11th, and 3rd, then also, the illness will be cured.

On the Curse of Deities

वह्वयङ्कद्वादशे षष्ठे लग्नात्पापग्नहो यदि ।
हतो गदैर्जलैश्शस्त्रैस्तस्य दोष: कुलोद्भद: ॥ ६३ ॥

Stanza 63: If malefics are in Apoklimas, the disease is hereditary having been caused by water or instruments.

NOTES

Apoklimas are 3, 6, 9 and 12. Malefic planets in these places indicate that the disease, from which the querent or the person on whose behalf the query is put, will be due to inherited factors though the immediate cause may appear to be accumulation of liquids in the affected parts or cuts due to instruments.

प्रेताश्च राहौ, पितर: सुरेज्ये, चन्द्रेऽम्बुदेव्यस्तपनेऽपि देव्य: ।
स्वगोत्रदेव्यश्च शनौ बुधे च भूतानि विन्द्याद्व्ययरन्ध्रसंस्थे ॥ ६४ ॥

शाकिन्य आरे भृगुजेऽम्बुदेव्यो गृह्, नन्ति मर्त्यं विमुखंसुकुन्दात् ।
स्वर्क्षेच्चगे वीर्ययुते च साध्याश्चन्द्रे च नीचे विबले
                                       न साध्या ॥ ६५ ॥

केन्द्रे स्थंबलिभि: पापैरसाध्या देवतागणा: ।
सौम्यग्रहैश्च केन्द्रस्थै: साध्या मन्त्रस्तवार्चनै: ॥ ६६ ॥

Stanzas 64 to 66: According as the planets occupying the 8th or 12th are Rahu, Jupiter, the Moon, the Sun, Saturn, Mercury, Mars and Venus the sickness or disease will be due to the *pretas*, curses of parents, a deity frequenting watery places, a female deity, family deity, spirits of dead persons, a *sakini* and a watery deity respectively. These deities possess athiests. When the Moon is strongly disposed in exaltation or own house, the disease can be cured; otherwise, the disease cannot be cured. When strong malefics are in quadrants, even when the deities are propitiated, relief is not possible. If benefics are in Kendras, *mantras* and *japas* will help.

When the Moon is in an Upachaya and benefics occupy quadrants, trines or the 8th, and the ascendant is aspected by benefics, the sick man will be relieved of his sickness.

NOTES

Stanza 64 to 66 give combinations for knowing the cause of disease brought about by factors other than organic. The belief is still widely held that the spirits of dead persons and female and male deities are responsible for bringing about diseases which are of a psychosomatic nature. I do not propose to enlarge upon the rationale of belief in such things.

Researches in psychical phenomena made in Europe and America have been lending strong confirmation to the theory that the human personality survives physical death and that depending upon the nature and inclination of one's existence in the physical life, the personality after death assumes different types of existence favouring or persecuting their near and dear ones according to the harmonious and hostile relationships they had with the affected persons, while living on the earth.

A *preta* is a disembodied soul soon after death. It is said that the course of a *preta* towards a higher plane of existence depends on the satisfactory performance of the obsequies by the sons or dependents of the deceased concerned. When these ceremonies are not properly performed the *preta* is denied safe conduct with the result curses are sent to the persons responsible for such omission.

Bhutas are different spirits or disembodied souls frustrated in their earth-life.

Ambadevis are female deities resident in watery places.

Devi mentioned in stanza 64 is interpreted by the commentator as a female *preta* or disembodied spirit. Swagotradevi is the family deity.

Sakini is a female divinity of an inferior character attendant specially on Siva and Durga.

If the planet oecupying the 8th or 12th is Rahu, the disease in due to *pretas*; Jupiter—parents; the Moon—Ambadevi; the Sun—Devi; Saturn—family deity; Mercury—Bhutas; Mars—Sakini; and Venus—Ambadevi.

The subject of "deities" causing diseases is fascinating and I have dealt with it exhaustively in my English translation of *Prasna Marga*.

कण्टकाष्टत्रिकोणस्थाः शुभा उपचये शशी ।
लग्ने च शुभसन्दृष्टे रोगी रोगाद्विमुच्यते ॥ ६७ ॥

Stanza 67: The sick person will be cured of his sickness when benefics are in Kendras, Trikonas and the 8th; the Moon is in an Upachaya and the Lagna is aspected by benefics.

NOTES

According to this stanza, benefics should occupy 1, 4, 7, 10, 8, 5 and 9th, the Moon must be in 3, 6, 10, or 11 and the ascendant should be subjected to the aspect of benefic planets.

Master-Servant Relations

शीर्षोदये सौम्ययुते क्षिते वा सौम्यैर्द्वितीयाष्टमसप्तमस्थैः ।
तृतीयलाभारिगतैश्च पापैः सौख्यार्थलाभो नृपसेवकस्य ॥ ६८ ॥

Stanza 68: The master-servant relationship will be cordial and beneficial if the ascendant is a Sirshodaya sign occupied or aspected by benefic planets; benefics are placed in the 2nd, 7th and 8th; and malefics occupy the 3rd, 6th and 11th.

NOTES

This and the following three stanzas are from *Trailokya Prakuska*. For good relations to exist between master and servant—and this includes proprietor and worker, employer and employee as well, a Sirshodaya Sign (Gemini, Leo, Virgo, Libra, Scorpio or Aquarius) should rise, occupied or aspected by benefic planets; or benefics should be disposed in the 2nd, 7th and 8th and malefics in the 3rd, 6th and 11th.

लग्नाद्द्वितीये मदनाष्टमर्क्षे वित्तक्षयं सम्भ्रममार्तिमृत्युम् ।
कुर्वन्ति पापाः क्रमशो नरेन्द्रादभृत्यस्य
तस्मात्परिवर्जयेत्तम् ॥ ६९ ॥

Stanza 69: According as malefics occupy the ascendant, the 2nd, the 7th or 8th, the servant will suffer from loss of money, mental affliction, difficulties and death respectively in the hands of the ruler (or employer). Hence he should reject such a master.

NOTES

The question is generally put before one accept service. Therefore if at the time of query, the planetary dispositions are such as mentioned in stanza 69, it is advisable for the person not to enter the service of the employer (king, master, etc.) because if employed under him it will be to his detriment by way of financial trouble, mental affliction, difficulties and even death.

In answering such questions, a literal application of the original is not advisable.

The question may also relate to the advisability or otherwise of continuing in the service, the querent may be in, for the time being.

लग्नाद्वितीयाष्टमसप्तमर्क्षाः पापाः प्रणाशं नृपभृत्ययोर्द्वयोः ।
कुर्वन्ति तेष्वेवगताश्च सौम्याः कुर्युर्धनारोग्यसुखानि
चोभयोः ॥ ७० ॥

Stanza 70: It will be to the detriment to the interests of both the employer and the employee if malefics occupy the ascendant, 2nd, 7th and 8th. Benefics in these places conduce to the well-being of both the parties.

शशाङ्कसौम्यैरुदयास्तभावौ दृष्टौ युतो वा सबलैर्न पापैः ।
प्रष्टुस्तदा स्याद्धृदि पार्थिवस्य
स्नेहप्रसादादकृपाप्रतीपात् ॥ ७१ ॥

Stanza 71: If the Moon and benefic planets occupy or aspect the ascendant and the 7th unafflicted by powerful malefics, the employer will take to the querent with kindness and friendliness.

Future With Another Master

षष्ठेश्वरेण व्ययपेन केन्द्रे यदीत्थशालं कुरुते विलग्नपः ।
प्रष्टुस्तदाऽन्यः प्रभुरर्थदः स्यादतः प्रतीपान्न भवेत्परः प्रभुः ॥ ७२ ॥

Stanza 72: When the lord of the ascendant occupying a quadrant has an Ithasala with the lord of the 6th or 12th, the querent will benefit from another master. If contrarily disposed, there will be no benefit.

NOTES

The question is: Will I have a future with another master or employer? This implies a change of the present employer. The answer should be that the querent will be financially benefited under his new master. This implies also that he will leave the present job.

If there is no Ithasala between the lord of the ascendant—he should occupy a Kendra—and the lord of the 6th or 12th, then it is not advisable to change the present job.

This particular combination has been found to be correct in our humble experience. If the lord of the Lagna is in a Chara Rasi (moveable sign), there will also be change of place. Otherwise it will only be a change of the present employer.

लग्नेश्वरे स्वर्क्षगते स्वतुङ्गकेन्द्रस्थिते शीतकरेत्थशाले ।
शुभग्रहैर्दृष्टयुते बलान्विते प्रष्टुनिजस्वाम्यमितार्थलाभः ॥ ७३ ॥

Stanza 73: The querent will secure improvement in the present job itself if the lord of the ascendant occupies a Kendra, identical with his exaltation or own house and is in Ithasala with the Moon and is otherwise strongly disposed and unafflicted.

NOTES

The prime condition is the *par excellence* strength on the ascendant-lord and his being in Ithasala with the Moon. Further prospects in the existing position are denoted.

जायेश्वरे स्वोच्चनिजर्क्षसंस्थे केन्द्रस्थिते शीतकरेत्थशालगे ।
शुभग्रहैर्दृष्टयुते बलोत्कटः प्रष्टुस्तदाऽन्यः प्रभुरर्थदो
भवेत् ॥ ७४ ॥

Stanza 74: If the lord of the 7th is situated in a Kendra identical with his exaltation or own house and has Ithasala with the Moon and fortified by benefic aspects and association, the querent will immensely benefit under his new employer.

NOTES

This implies change of the present job. The Lagna indicates the present employer. The 7th indicates the next employer.

इदं गृहं वा शुभमन्यदालयं स्थानन्त्विदं वा शुभमन्यदालयम् ।
ममात्र भद्रं गमनात्तु तत्र वा पृष्ठोदयोत्थं विधिना विमृश्य ॥ ७५ ॥

Stanza 75: If a query "will I prosper in this house or in this place or elsewhere" is put, say he will get on well if a Prishtodaya sign rises. Predict after taking into account all the pros and cons.

NOTES

The stanza is clear and needs no further elucidation.

Recovery of Lost Property

प्रश्ने चतुर्थाधिपतिस्तत्रस्थे चाऽवलोकिते ।
अवश्यं वर्तते तत्र धनं चन्द्रेऽथ वा वदेत् ॥ ७६ ॥

Stanza 76: If the lord of the 4th is in the ascendant or the Moon is in the ascendant, aspected by the lord of the 4th, the lost money is to be found in the expected place.

NOTES

The questions concern the recovery of lost wealth or hidden wealth. In ancient times when there were no. banks, one's wealth was usually kept buried and with the death of the person, knowledge of where it was buried was lost. These astrological principles were perhaps formulated to tackle such questions. They refer to nashtadravya or lost wealth.

वित्तपे धनगे बन्धौ वाऽस्ति तत्र धनं बहु ।
पापे तुर्यगते द्रव्यं तूर्णे न लभ्यते ॥ ७७ ॥

Stanza 77: If the lord of the 2nd is in the 2nd or 4th, he will have access to much wealth. If malefics are in the 4th, he will get no wealth.

NOTES

Lost wealth can be retrieved when the combination given in the 1st part of the stanza is present. If malefics are in the 4th, the lost money cannot be secured at all.

भौमे सप्ताष्टराशिस्थे धनमन्यत्र नाप्यते ।
लग्ने तमो रविरिछिद्रे तदा द्रव्यं न लभ्यते ॥ ७८ ॥
(सप्ताष्टदशपातालेशो विधुर्धनदो गुरुः) ॥ ७८ ॥

Stanza 78: When Mars is in the 7th or 8th, the wealth will not be secured by the querent as it will be in the protection of another person. If Rahu is in the ascendant and the Sun is in the 8th, the wealth or property will not be secured. The wealth can be secured if cither the Moon or Jupiter becomes the lord of the 7th, 8th, 4th or 10th.

NOTES

This combination, can also be applied to know whether a minor's property left in the hands of a trustee could be got back or not. If Mars is in the 7th or 8th, then the trustee will have transferred it to others and the minor when he attains the majority may not get it back. Questions of a similar nature—getting back mortgaged property, etc.—can be successfully answered by adapting the combinations given in this stanza.

The last part of the stanza—the Moon of Jupiter owning the 4th, 10th, 8th or 7th appears to be either an interpolation or an after-thought as it is not in the body of the stanza but in parenthesis.

लग्नेश्वरे द्यूनगते विलग्ने जायेश्वरे नष्टधनस्य लाभः ।
जायेशलग्नाधिपतीत्थशाले द्यूने विनष्टं धनमेति मर्त्यः ॥ ७९ ॥

Stanza 79: The lost wealth will be got back if the lords of Lagna and the 7th are in the 7th and Lagna respectively. Similar result will happen if the two lords are in Ithasala in the 7th.

लग्नेशजायाधिपतीत्थशाले लग्नेश्वरं यच्छति तस्करोऽर्थम् ।
सूर्ये विलग्नेऽस्तमिते शशाङ्के न लभ्यते यद्द्रविणं,
विनष्टम् ॥ ८० ॥

Stanza 80: When the lords of the ascendant and the 7th are in Ithasala, the latter transfers his influence to the former, meaning the thief will return the wealth. When the Sun is in the ascendant and the Moon is in the 7th, the lost wealth will not be recovered.

NOTES

In stanza 79, the meaning implies that the stolen money will be recovered if there is Ithasala in the 7th between the lord of the 1st and 7th. The first part of stanza 80 exemplifies this further by suggesting that because the 7th lord transfers his influence when in Ithasala with the lord of the ascendant, the stolen property will be returned by the thief himself. When the query is on a full Moon day at about the time of sunrise the property will not be recovered.

कर्मेशलग्नाधिपतीत्थशाले चौरः स्वमादाय पुरात्पलायते ।
चन्द्रेऽस्तपे चार्ककरप्रविष्टे तल्लभ्यते नष्टधनं सतस्करम् ॥ ८१ ॥

Stanza 81: The thief will himself steal the property and run away to his abode, when there is Ithasala between the lords of the 1st and 10th houses. The thief will be caught with the stolen property if the Moon and the lord of the 7th are in combustion.

NOTES

Ithasala between lords of the 1st and the 10th indicates that the lost property will not be secured. If the lord of the 7th is in combustion and the Moon and the Sun are within 12°, the culprit will be caught red-handed.

अस्तश्वरे केन्द्रगतेऽस्ति चौरस्ततैव, वाऽन्यत्र पुराद्विनिर्गत: ।
धर्मेशदुश्चिक्यपतीत्थशाले जायेश्वरेऽन्यत्र गत:
स चौर: ॥ ८२ ॥

Stanza 82: The thief is in the place of theft if the lord of the 7th is in a quadrant. He will have bolted away from the place if the 7th lord is in any other place. If the lord of the 7th is in Ithasala with the lord of the 3rd or 9th, the thief will have left the town limits.

कर्मेशलग्नाधिपतीत्थशाले यल्लभ्यते राजकुलाच्च चौर्यम् ।
विधमंपद्यून पतीत्थशाले त्वन्यप्रदेशाद्गमने तदाप्ति: ॥ ८३ ॥

Stanza 83: When the lord of 10th is in Ithasala with the lord of the ascendant, recovery of the stolen property will be through the police. If either the lord of the 3rd or the lord of the 9th has Ithasala with the lord of the 7th, the property will be recovered in another place.

शुभेत्थशाले हिमगौ विलग्ने खस्थेऽथ वा नष्टधनस्य लाभ: ।
सुस्नेहदृष्ट्या रविणा शुभेन दृष्टे विलग्ने हिमगौ
च लाभ: ॥ ८४ ॥

Stanza 84: The property will be recovered if the Moon occupying the ascendant or the 10th is in benefic Ithasala. If such a Moon has a friendly aspect from the Sun or a benefic planet, then also the property will be got back.

NOTES

Stanzas 82 to 84 furnish interesting information on lost property, how it is secured and whether the thief is within the limits of the town, where the crime is committed or whether he has left the place, etc. The 3rd and 9th houses signify going out of the place and the 10th, the hand of the authority, viz., the police. We do not think these stanzas call for an elaborate explanation as they are clear to understand. By friendly aspect is meant a trine, a sextile or a conjunction (provided the conjoined planets happen to be benefics).

स्थिरोदये स्थिरांशे वा वर्गोत्तमगतेऽपि वा ।
स्थितं तत्रैव तद्द्रव्यं स्वकीयेनैव चोरितम् ॥ ८५ ॥

Stanza 85: If a fixed sign or a fixed Navamsa rises, or the Lagna is Vargottama, the thief will be the querent's own man and the property will be with him.

आदिमध्यावसानेषु द्रेष्काणेषु विलग्नतः ।
द्वारदेशे तथा मध्ये गृहान्ते च वदेद्धनम् ॥ ८६ ॥

Stanza 86: According as the rising Drekkana is the first, the middle or the last, the lost property will respectively be hidden near the door, or inside the premises, or in the backyard of the house.

NOTES

Stanzas 85 and 86 are from *Shat Panchasikha*. I would refer the readers to the English translation of this great work, by my revered grandfather late Prof. B. Suryanarain Rao.

पतितधनस्थप्रश्ने मिथो गृहस्थौ विलग्नसप्तेशौ ।
यदि मुथशिलन्तयोः स्यासदाऽऽशुतत्रैव वदति धनम् ॥ ८७ ॥

Stanza 87: If the question refers to money inadvertently lost, say that it is in the place dropped if the lord of the ascendant is in the 7th and *vice versa* or if both the lords are in Muthasila.

नष्टं क्व दिशि प्राप्तं ? पृच्छायां लग्नगे विधौ प्राच्याम् ।
खस्थाने याम्यायामस्ते वारुण्यां वा भुव्युदोच्याम् ॥ ८८ ॥

Stanza 88: If "In which direction is the lost property to be secured" is the question, say that it is in the east, south, west or north according as the Moon occupies the ascendant, the 10th, the 7th or the 4th house.

यदि नेन्दः केन्द्रे तच्चत्वारिंशांशकैश्च पञ्चयुतैः ।
भागे दिक्क्रम उक्तो, वह्नयवनीवायुवारिराशौ वा ॥। ८९ ॥

Stanza 89: When the Moon is not in a Kendra, the direction is signified by his position from the nearest quadrant, the reckoning commencing from the ascendant as east and every 45° therefrom representing a cardinal point in the order of east, south-east, southwest, north, north-west and north-east; or the direction is signified by the nature of the rising sign.

NOTES

Suppose the ascendant is 12° Aries and the Moon is, say in 8° Virgo. Here the nearest Kendra or quadrant is the 7th, the Moon being 34° behind. The ascendant (Aries 12°) represents the east, the 7th (Libra 12°) represents west. The 4th (Cancer 12°) rules the north and the 10th (Capricorn 12°) represents the south.

The Moon is between the IV (north) and the VII (west) but more than 45° from the 4th. Hence the direction is west. If supposing the Moon were exactly 45° from the 4th, then the direction would have been north-west.

Suppose the ascendant is 20° Cancer and the Moon is in Virgo 5°. The ascendant represents the east, and the 4th represents the north. 45° indicates northeast. If supposing the Moon was in 10° Virgo which means nearer the 4th house and hence the direction will be north.

Another method is also given. If the rising sign is fiery, the direction is south-east; if earthy, southwest; if airy, north-west and if watery, north-east. To put it more clearly, this formula is also to be applied when the Moon is not in a Kendra.

नष्टचीतवित्तलब्धे: पृच्छायां चौरसप्तमं ततो लाभ: ।
हिब्बुकं द्रव्यस्थानं लग्नं चन्द्रश्च धननाथ: ॥ ९० ॥

Stanza 90: In regard to questions bearing on lost or stolen wealth, 7th signifies the thief, the 4th signifies the property and the ascendant and the Moon signify the person, who has lost the money.

लग्नेशोऽस्तेऽस्तपतिना चेन्मुथशिली ततो लाभ: ।
यद्यष्टेशो लग्ने तदा स्वयं तस्करोऽर्पयति ॥ ९१ ॥

Stanza 91: The lost property will be recovered if the lord of the Lagna is in the 7th in Ithasala with the 7th lord. The thief himself will return the property when the lord of the 8th is in the ascendant.

रविरश्मिगे धनेशे वाऽस्तमिते तस्करस्य लाभ: स्यात् ।
लग्नेश दशमपत्योर्मुथशिलत: प्राप्यते स्ववान् चौर: ॥ ९२ ॥

Stanza 92: If the lord of the 2nd is combust, the thief will be caught. If the lords of the ascendant and the 10th are in Ithasala, the thief will be apprehended along with the property.

लग्नेशदृष्ट्यभावे चौर: सह मात्रया याति ।
अस्ताधिपतौ दग्धे रविरश्मिगतेऽथ लभ्यते चौर: ॥ ९३ ॥

Stanza 93: If in the above combination, there is no aspect of the lord of Lagna, the thief will have come just for committing the theft. If the lord of the 7th is combust, the thief will be caught.

लग्नपकृतेत्थाले राजभयाद्धनमिदं स्वयं दत्ते ।
लग्नास्तपयोर्न स्याद्यदि दृष्टिलंग्नपस्तथा विकल: ॥ ९४ ॥

तत्तस्करोऽस्य हस्ताद्ददाति चौर्ये हि राजकुले ।
लग्नपमध्यपयोगे राजकुलं प्राप्य लभ्यते चौर्यम् ॥ ९५ ॥

Stanzas 94 and 95: When there is Ithasala between the lords of the ascendant and the 7th, the money will be returned by the thief due to the fear of the police. When there is no Ithasala and when the lord of the ascendant is weak, the thief returns the money to the authorities concerned. When the lords of the 1st and 10th are in conjunction, the stolen property can be got by going to the authorities.

NOTES

Stanzas 94 and 95 comprehend three factors:

- (a) The property being automatically returned to the querent by the thief because of fear of authority—Ithasala must be present between lords of the ascendant and the 7th.

- (b) The property being returned to the police—no Ithasala mentioned in (a) and lord of Lagna weak.

- (c) The property can be secured from the authorities, which means the thief will have been apprehended and condition (b) must be present—the lord of the 1st and the 10th in conjunction. That is, to get the property from the authorities, there should be no Ithasala between the lords of the Lagna and the 7th, the lord of the Lagna must be weak but he should. be in conjunction with the lord of the 10th.

रन्ध्रं चौरस्य धनं धनपे तनाथ सप्तमे नाप्ति: ।
रन्ध्रपतौ धनपस्य तु सुथशिलयोगे च प्राप्यते वित्तम् ॥ ९६ ॥

Stanza 96: The thief's money is signified by the 8th house. If the lord of the 2nd is. in the 7th or 8th, the stolen property will not be recovered. If there is Muthasila between the lords of the 2nd and 9th, the money will be got back..

रन्ध्रपतौ दशमपतेर्मुथशिलगे चौरपक्षकृद्भूप: ।
धनपे विलग्नपे सति दृष्टिविहीने श्रुतिर्भवति नाप्ति: ॥ ९७ ॥

Stanza 97: When there is Muthasila between the lords of the 8th and the 10th, the authority will favour the thief's point of view. When there is no mutual aspect between the lords of the ascendant and the 2nd, the querent will get news about lost property, but he will not recover it.

NOTES

Combinations for getting back and not getting back the lost property are given in stanza 96. According to stanza 97, the culprit will be known but the culprit will himself be the beneficiary due to wrong judgment on the part of the police; or the police may side the thief and the querent will not get the money. This is possible when the lords of the 8th and the 10th are in Muthasila. On the other hand, when the lords of the 1st and the 2nd have no mutual aspect, news may come about the thief but the money will not be recovered.

चौरज्ञानप्रश्ने लग्नरविशशिदृशा स्वगृहचौरः ।
अनयोरेकदृशा गृहसमीपवर्ती वसत्येषः ॥ ९८ ॥

Stanza 98: If the query is "who is the thief", say he is a member in the household of the querent if the ascendant is aspected by the Sun or the Moon. If both the Sun and the Moon aspect the Lagna, then say the thief lives near the querent's house.

NOTES

The combined aspect of the Sun and the Moon is possible only when they are together, which means new moon day or a day earlier or later.

लग्नस्थे लग्नपतावस्तपयुक्ते च गृहगतश्चौरः ।
अस्ताधिपतावन्त्ये सहजे वा स्वीयभृत्योऽयम् ॥ ९९ ॥

Stanza 99: When the lords, of the ascendant and the 7th are in the ascendant, the thief is one belonging to the same household. If the lord of the 7th is in the 12th or the 3rd, the thief is the querent's own servant.

अस्तेशे तुङ्गस्थे स्वगृहे वा तस्करः प्रसिद्धः स्यात् ।
लग्नदशमास्तभावाः क्रमेण वीक्ष्याः स्वतुङ्गभवनादौ ।
यः खेटः स्याद्बलवान् स ज्ञेयस्तस्करस्य बली ॥ १०० ॥

Stanza 100: The thief is a well-known person if the lord of the 7th occupies his own or exaltation place. He will have been assisted by a person signified by the strongest of planets occupying the ascendant, the 7th or the 10th.

NOTES

The 7th rules the thief. If the lord of the 7th is exalted, he will be a notorious person. Examine carefully the ascendant, the 7th and the 10th houses and find which of the planets posited in these three places is the strongest as judged by occupation of exalted or own house. A person appropriate to the physical and mental characteristics of this planet will have assisted the thief in committing the crime.

एवं योगं तु विना द्यूनेशस्यैव बलमभिग्राह्यम् ।
इत्थं चौरज्ञाने चौर: सूर्ये, गृहेश्वरस्य पिता ॥ १०१ ॥

Stanza 101: When the combinations given above are present, judge the thief by the strength of the lord of the 7th. If such a planet happens to be debilitated Sun, the father of the houseowner will be the thief.

चन्द्रे माता, शुक्रे भार्या, मन्दे सुतो भवेन्नीचे ।
जीवे गृहप्रधानं भौमे पुत्रोऽथ वा भ्राता ॥ १०२ ॥

Stanza 102: According as such a debilitated planet happens to be the Moon, Venus, Saturn, Jupiter or Mars, the thief will respectively be the owner's mother, wife, son, an important member of the house or brother or the son.

NOTES

The lord of the 7th must be debilitated to indicate the person described in the above stanza. For Mars, the thief could be either a brother or a son. The other descriptions are clear.

ज्ञे स्वजनो मित्रं वा ज्ञात्वेत्थं पुण्यसहममादेश्यम् ।
तस्मिन् क्रुरादृष्टे पुरा न चौरोऽस्तपे पुराऽपि स्यात् ॥ १०३ ॥

Stanza 103: If the debilitated lord of the 7th is Mercury, then the thief will be a relative or a friend. The nature of the thief should also be ascertained by a consideration of *Punyasaham*. If the *Punyasaham* is not aspected by malefics, the thief determined as above will not be the thief. But if the 7th lord is aspected by malefics, the earlier finding holds good.

NOTES

Some explanation is necessary. Suppose as per stanza 102, the lord of the 7th happens to be Saturn and he is debilitated Then you have to suspect the son of the house-owner for theft. If suppose the Punyasaham calculated for the time of query is not aspected by malefics, then the son will not be the thief. If, however, Saturn (lord of the 7th) is aspected by a malefic, then the thief will be a son. If Saturn is not aspected by a malefic but Punyasaham is aspected by a malefic, then also, the thief will be a son.

In all these cases, the thief may or may not have directly committed the theft. He might have got it done through an agent of his.

अस्तेशान्मूसरिफे भौमे चौरः पुराऽपि निगृहीतः ।
सप्तेशे रविपुत्रे चन्द्रदृशा तस्करो हि पाखण्डी ॥ १०४ ॥

Stanza 104: When the lord of the 7th is in Musaripha with Mars, the thief will not have been caught before. If Saturn happening to be the lord, of the 7th is aspected by the Moon, the thief is an heretic.

NOTES

Mars and the lord of the 7th in Musaripha denotes that the thief is not a professional or he has not been apprehended for theft hitherto. He will be a *pakhandi* or heretic if the Moon aspects Saturn who should be lord of the 7th.

जीवो विलोक्य लोकं, भौमे खातेन पालकं भक्त्या ।
प्रतिकुञ्चिकयाऽपहृतं सितेऽतिथिज्ञें प्रपञ्चकरः ॥ १०५ ॥

Stanza 105: Jupiter denotes the crime being committed with public notice. Mars indicates the money being hidden in a pit. Venus suggests use of a duplicate key. Mercury denotes that the theft is due to a guest.

NOTES

The above results are said to happen when the lord of the 7th is aspected by the different planets.

I can recall a theft case that occurred in the office of a newspaper. The chart showed lord of the 7th being aspected by Jupiter and Mars. It was revealed that the theft was committed in the presence of other employees by the use of a duplicate key. The culprit was caught and dismissed. It became known that being himself an employee he opened the room with a duplicate key and removed some small but costly lino machine spare parts. The other employees did not notice the theft being committed.

चौरस्य वयोज्ञाने सिते युवा, ज्ञे शिशुर्गुरौ मध्यः
तरुणो भौमे, मन्दे वृद्धोऽर्के स्यादतिस्थविरः ॥ १०६ ॥

Stanza 106: According as the significator happens to be Venus, Mercury, Jupiter, Mars, Saturn or the Sun, the thief will respectively be a youth, a boy, a middle-aged person, a young person, an old man and a very old person.

रविनभयो: स्वमन्दिरे स्मरभूमिलग्नयोर्मध्यम् ।
चरति रवौ नवमध्यमवृद्धवयोऽतीतका: क्रमश: ॥ १०७॥

Stanza 107: If the Sun is in the 12th or 2nd, the thief is a young person. If the sign is Leo, the thief is of middle age. If the Sun is in the 7th, he is old and if in the 4th, very old.

NOTES

The above two stanzas enable us to ascertain the age of the thief by noting which planet is the ruler of the 7th thus: Venus—a youth or teen-ager; Mercury—a boy: Jupiter—a middle-aged person; Mars—a well-built young person; Saturn—an old man; and the Sun—a very old man.

Stanza 106 gives another method based on the position of the Sun. But this is not found very reliable in our humble experience. Another interpretation put on this Yoga is, if the Sun is between:

10th and 12th, the thief is a boy;

1st to 3rd: young;

4th to 6th very old; and

7th to 9th: old.

According to a Pandit whom I met at Jaipur both the stanzas should be combined to find the age of the thief thus: For example, if the lord of the 7th is Jupiter, the thief (as per stanza 106) is a middle-aged person. Decide his exact age by noting the position of the Sun. If, suppose, the Sun is in the 8th, then he will be old in the range of "middle age". I cannot vouch safe for the reliability of this interpretation but it is worthwhile testing it.

Students of astrology are to be cautioned that in determining the thief or his age, they have to be careful. It is not merely the significator of the thief (lord of the 7th) that is to be considered but also the influence he is subject to and his exact position in the sign occupied. The avasthas of planets (*vide Hindu Predictive Astrology.* Chapter VII) will help in determining the age within the age-group allotted to different planets.

नष्टस्थाने प्रश्ने तुर्ये भूम्यग्निवायुजलमध्यात् ।
यो भवति राशिरस्मात्स्थानं ज्ञेयं गतधनस्य ॥ १०८ ॥

Stanza 108: The place, where the stolen article is kept, will be appropriate to the nature of the sign in the fourth house—earthy, fiery, airy or watery.

NOTES

If the sign is earthy, the spot is a floor; if fiery, near a place of fire; airy—somewhere above; watery—near a watery place. Here the karakatwas of signs will be helpful. A fiery sign may indicate the kitchen, furnace, a place of smelter, etc.

अथ चतुर्थगृहे तुर्येश्वरोऽथ यः स्याद्ग्रहस्ततो ज्ञेयम् ।
मन्दे मलिनस्थाने, चन्द्रऽम्बुनि, गोष्पतौ सुरारामे ॥ १०९ ॥

भौमे वह्निसमीपे, रवो गृहाधीश्वरासनस्थाने ।
तल्पे शुक्रे, सौम्ये पुस्तकवित्तान्नयानपार्श्वे च ॥ ११० ॥

Stanzas 109 and 110: The nature of the planet owning or occupying the 4th should also be considered. If the planet is Saturn—a dirty place; the Moon—watery place; Jupiter—temples; Mars—near fire; the Sun—the principal seat of the owner in his house; Venus—bed; Mercury—place where food is served or library or money is kept.

NOTES

Stanzas 109 and 110 give more details about the place where the stolen article may have been deposited. Here the nature of the planets concerned is considered. According as the planet influencing the fourth house is Saturn, the Moon, Jupiter, Mars, the Sun, Venus, or Mercury, the stolen article will have been hidden in a place where dirt is collected; near a well; bathroom, etc.; temple or prayer room; kitchen or place where fire is used; near the seat of the owner; a bed; a dining hall, library, treasury or an iron safe.

Identity of Thief

चौरोऽयमथ न वेति क्रूरेन्द्रोर्मुथशिले च चौरः स्यात् ।
सौम्यशशिमुथशिले खलु न भवति चौरः प्रवक्तव्यम् ॥ १११ ॥

Stanza 111: If the question "is he the thief or not" is put, say that the suspected person is the thief if there is Muthasila between the Moon and a malefic. If the Moon's Muthasila is with benefics, the suspected person is not the thief.

किमनेन तस्करत्वं कदाऽपि विहितं न वेति-पृच्छायाम् ।
लग्नपशशिनोरेकस्मादपि मूसरिफेऽस्तपे विहितम् ॥ ११२ ॥

Stanza 112: If "has he committed any theft before" is the question, say that he has committed a theft before if either the Moon or the ascendant lord is in Musaripha, with the lord of the 7th.

NOTES

The combinations given in stanzas 111 and 112 enable us to say clearly whether or not a suspected person is the real thief and whether if he is not the thief at the present occasion, he has in the past committed any thefts.

The Moon's Muthasila with a benefic absolves the suspect from the charge of thieving. The Moon's Muthasila with a malefic confirms that the suspected person is the real thief. The suspect can however be considered to have committed a theft on a previous occasion if the ascendant lord or the Moon is in Musaripha with the lord of the 7th.

चौरः स्त्री पुरुषो वा पृच्छायामस्तपे स्त्रियो राशौ ।
स्त्रीखेटे स्वीदृष्टे चौर स्त्री व्यत्ययात्पुरुषः ॥ ११३॥

Stanzas 113: If the lord of the 7th is a feminine planet or is in a feminine sign or is joined with or aspected by feminine planets, the thief is a female. If contrary, the thief is a male.

NOTES

Mercury, Venus, Saturn and the Moon are female planets. The Sun, Mars and Jupiter are male planets. If the lord of the 7th is a male planet or the 7th is a male sign or is joined with or aspected by a male planet, the thief is a male.

All odd signs are masculine and all even signs are feminine.

लग्नेश्वरनवमांशतो वय: प्रमाणजातथो ज्ञेया: ।
चौरोऽयमिहानन्तं शास्त्रं कथितोऽयमुद्देश: ॥ ११४ ॥

Stanza 114: By carefully studying the Navamsa dispositions of the ascendant lord, ascertain the age, size, caste, etc., of the thief. Of the plenty of literature available on the subject of identifying the thief, I have explained a few principles here.

SPECIAL RULES REGARDING CHILDREN

लग्नेश्वरेणाथ निशाकरेण यदोत्थशालं कुरुते सुतेश: ।
शुभ: शुभै: संयुत ईक्षित: स्यात् स सन्तति प्रष्टुरसौ
                                    विदध्यात् ॥ ११५ ॥

Stanza 115: If the lord of the 5th is in Ithasala with either the lord of the ascendant or the Moon and is associated with or aspected by benefics, the querent will have children.

पुंस्त्रीग्रहा: पुत्रगृहं बिलग्नात्पश्यन्ति यावन्ति इहातिवीर्या: ।
तत्संख्यका: स्युस्तनयाश्च कन्या:
                 शुभेशयोगात्सुतभांश-तुल्या: ॥ ११६ ॥

Stanza 116: The number of sons and daughters will correspond to the number of powerful masculine and feminine planets aspecting the 5th house; or the number of issues corresponds to the Navamsas gained by the 5th house, provided the 5th or its lord are in conjunction with benefics.

NOTES

In stanza 115, combination for predicting birth of issues is given. The condition is the lord of the 5th should be in Ithasala with the lord of the ascendant or the Moon. According to stanza 116, the number of issues, male and female, will be according to the number of strong male and female planets aspecting the 5th; or if the lord of the 5th is aspected by benefics note the number of amsas gained by the 5th house and that represents the number of issues. We are of the opinion that the number of navamsas gained by the lord of the 5th should be taken instead of the 5th house itself.

लग्नेशपुत्राधिपती परस्परं न पश्यतश्चदुदयं च पञ्चमम् ।
पापेथशालो सुतलग्नपौ च प्रष्टुस्तदा सन्ततिनासिततां
वदेत् ॥ ११७ ॥

Stanza 117: The querent can never have children when there is no mutual aspect between, the lords of the 1st and the 5th or the lord of the 1st does not aspect the 5th or vice versa or the lord of the 5th has Ithasala with malefics.

NOTES

Three combinations are given for denying the birth of children.

(1) No aspect between lords of the 1st and the 5th.

(2) Lord of the 1st does not aspect the 5th and lord of the 5th does not aspect the 1st.

(3) Lord of the 5th has Ithasala with malefic planets.

पुत्रालये सिंहवृषालिकन्या: प्रश्नोदयाज्जन्मभत स्तथेन्दो: ।
अल्पप्रज: सन्ततिपृच्छक: स्यात् पापै: सुतर्क्षे
                                     सहिते क्षिते वा ॥ ११८ ॥

Stanza 118: The querent will have very few number of issues if the 5th house happens to be Leo, Taurus, Scorpio or Virgo and the 5th house from the query ascendant or from the birth ascendant or from birth Moon are occupied or aspected by malefics.

स्वक्षं स्थितौ रन्ध्रगतौ यमको प्रष्ठु: स्त्रियं संदिशतश्च वन्ध्याम् ।
छिद्रस्थित चन्द्रबुधौ सदोषां वा कार्कवन्ध्यां तनया
                                     प्रसूतिम् ॥ ११९ ॥

Stanza 119: When the Sun or Saturn is in the 8th identical with his own sign, the querent's wife is a *vandhya*. If Mercury or the Moon is in the 8th, the querent will get a daughter.

NOTES

Combinations given in stanzas 118 and 119 are the same as given in standard books on predictive astrology but only the Prasna Lagna or ascendant at the time of query is introduced Saturn or the Sun in the 8th in own house is said to make the wife a *vandhya* or incapable of conceiving. When Mercury or the Moon is in the 8th (at the time of question) the birth of at least one daughter can be anticipated.

मृतप्रजा छिद्रगयो: सितेज्ज्ञयोर्गर्भत्रवां भूमिसुतेष्टमक्षैम् ।
छिद्रेश्वरे छिद्रगतेऽतिवीर्ये पुष्पं न विन्दत्यबला
                                     सुतप्रदम् ॥ १२० ॥

Stanza 120: The wife of the querent will deliver a dead child if the 8th is occupied by Jupiter or Venus.

On Special Questions

She will have abortion if Mars is in the 8th. If the strong lord of the 8th is in the 8th, the querent's wife cannot secrete the type of ovum that could be fertilized.

NOTES

The wife's inability to conceive due to a defect in the ovum is indicated by the presence of the lord of the 8th in the 8th. The other two combinations given in this stanza are clear. In this connection reference may be made to Bija and Kshetra Sphuta discussed in my book *How to Judge A Horoscope*.

शुक्रार्कयोरष्टमसंस्थयोर्वा क्रूरैर्धनान्त्याष्टमराशिसंस्थैः ।
जातः पुरस्तान्म्रियते प्रजा वै प्रष्टुर्न चाग्रे शुभसन्ततिः
स्यात् ॥ १२१ ॥

Stanza 121: When the 8th is occupied by the Sun or Venus or the 2nd, 12th and 8th are occupied by malefics, the first issue will die and subsequent issues also will not be long-lived.

रिष्फेश्वरे केन्द्रगते च सौम्यैर्युते क्षिते जीवति बालकश्च ।
आपूर्यमाणे शुभयुक्त इन्दौ केन्द्रे विशुजींवति
दीर्घकालम् ॥ १२२ ॥

Stanza 122: If the lord of the 12th is in a quadrant aspected by or associated with benefics, the child survives. If the full Moon with beneficial aspects are in a quadrant, then the child will be long-lived.

NOTES

The combinations given in stanzas 121 and 122 are clear enough and do not require elucidation.

पञ्चशोऽथ लग्नेशो विषमर्क्षगतौ यदा ।
पुत्रजन्मप्रदो ज्ञेयो कन्यानां समराशिगौ ॥ १२३ ॥

Stanza 123: When the lord of Lagna and the 5th are in odd signs, male issues will be born. When they are in even signs, daughters will be born.

सुताधिपे नृराशिस्थे पुंराशिस्थोऽपि लग्नपः ।
वीक्ष्यते पत्रदः प्रोक्तो युग्मराशौ च दारिकाः ॥ १२४ ॥

Stanza 124: The issue will be a male when the lord of the 5th is in a masculine sign and the lord of the Lagna is also in the 5th aspected by male planets. When the lord of the 5th house is in an even sign and the lord of the ascendant is also in an even sign aspected by female planets, the querent will have daughters.

युग्मराशिगते लग्ने यदा तत्र शुभग्रहाः ।
गर्भेऽपत्यद्वयं वाच्यं दैवज्ञेन विपश्चिता ॥ १२५ ॥

Stanza 125: When the ascendant is a common sign and happens to be occupied by benefics, twins will be born.

विषमोपगतो लग्नाच्छनिः पुत्र सुखप्रदः ।
समभे योषितां जन्म विशेषो जातकोक्तिवत् ॥ १२६ ॥

Stanza 126: When Saturn occupies an odd place counted from the ascendant, the querent will have male issues. If Saturn is in an even place from the ascendant, he will have daughters. What is to be noted is, further details should be gathered from books on predictive astrology.

NOTES

The above four stanzas are from *Prasna Chintamani* quoted by Neelakantha. They give combinations for predicting the birth of male and female children and twins. We are also advised to refer to other books on predictive astrology for more details about birth of issues, their sex, etc. Even according to *Prasna Marga*, combinations given in predictive astrology can be utilised for Prasna and *vice versa*.

On Meals

कटुको लवणस्तिक्तो मिश्रितो मधुरो रसः ।
कम्लः कषायः कथिता रव्यादीनां रसा बुधैः ॥ १२७ ॥

Stanza 127: The Sun and other planets signify respectively the tastes katuka (astringent), lavana (saltish), thikta (bitter), misrita (mixture of all tastes), madhura (sweet), amla (sour) and kashaya (bitter).

लग्नं पश्यति यः खेटस्तस्य यः कथितो रसः ।
भोजनेऽसौ रसो वीर्यक्रमद्घाच्याः परे रसाः ॥ १२८ ॥

Stanza 128: The strength of the planets aspecting the ascendant indicates the rasa or taste appropriate to it, which the person likes.

चन्द्रो यस्य मुथशिलस्तस्य विशेषं वन्देद्भुक्तौ ।
लग्ने राहौ मन्दे रविदृष्टे भोजनाभावः ॥ १२९ ॥

Stanza 129: He will have special liking for that taste which is signified by the planet in Muthasila with the Moon. The person will have to be starving if Rahu or Saturn is in the ascendant aspected by the Sun.

NOTES

In most Indian astrological works, different 'tastes' or flavours are assigned to different planets. Here by taste is meant, the flavour such as sweet, sour, etc., to which one has a liking. In Horary Astrology, we do not think that these combinations should have any importance other than academic.

One may have to face starvation for want of financial convenience if Rahu or Saturn is in the ascendant aspected by the Sun.

कीदृङ्मयाऽद्य भुक्तं ? पृच्छायां यदि भवेत्स्थिरं लग्नम् ।
तद्धुक्तमेकवेलं, द्व्यात्मनि वेलद्वयं चरे त्वसकृत् ॥ १३० ॥

Stanza 130: When a question 'what did I eat today' is put, say that the querent has eaten once, twice or many times according as the ascendant is a fixed, common or a moveable sign.

चन्द्रे लग्नगते स्यात्क्षारं, भौमे च कटुकमम्लगुरौ ।
मधुरं दिनकृति तिक्तं शुक्रे स्निग्धं बुधे च सर्वरसम् ॥ १३१ ॥

Stanza 131: According as the planet in the ascendant, is the Moon, Mars, Jupiter, the Sun, Venus or Mercury, he will have eaten the food tasting kshara (saltish), katuka (hot savoury), amla (sour), madhura (sweet), thikta (bitter) and a combination of all.

मन्दे कषायमशुभान्मुसरिफे शशिनि मुथशिले शुभेऽरिदृशा ।
उद्वाहात्प्रियदृष्ट्या प्रायणिकत्वात्समागतं भोज्यम् ॥ १३२ ॥

Stanza 132: When Saturn is in Lagna, the food will taste bitter (kashaya). When the Moon has Musaripha with a malefic and a hostile Ithasala with a benefic, he has attended a marriage dinner; if the Moon's

Ithasala with the benefic is friendly, he has attended the dinner by invitation.

NOTES

The above three stanzas are intended to answer what type of food one has eaten if the query relates to that topic. He will eat foods, the predominant tastes of which will be to his liking, according to the planet influencing the ascendant. The Moon can have Musaripha and Ithasala. The Musaripha must be with a malefic. If the Ithasala is a hostile aspect with a benefic he has attended a marriage dinner; if the aspect is not hostile he will be a special invitee for the dinner.

I am afraid such questions can have no relevance to important problems which Horary Astrology is expected to tackle. At best, they are intended to be stunt or sensation-mongering.

चन्द्रस्य चेत्याच्छुभजेत्थशाले पापेसराफे च तदेतदुक्तम् ।
पापेसराफे च शुभेत्थशाले चन्द्रे तु भुक्तं
शुभमन्नमीशम् ॥ १३३ ॥

Stanza 133: When the Moon has Ithasala with a benefic and Isaripha with a malefic, the querent will have had a rich and sumptuous meals.

शुभेसराफे त्वशुभेत्थशाले चन्द्रे कदनं मधुसर्पिषो बिना ।
पापेत्थशालेऽथ खलेसराफे शक्यं न भोक्तुं परतोऽपि
लब्धम् ॥ १३४ ॥

Stanza 134: When the Moon has Isaripha with a benefic and Ithasala with a malefic he will have eaten a food which is without sweet taste and ghee but which is pungent. When both Ithasala and Isaripha are with malefics, the food will not be from another place.

चन्द्रे स्वनाथदृष्ट सुखभोजनमन्यथा कष्टात् ।
गुरुमथशिले सगौरवमर्केण सुथशिलेऽतिशुद्धि
तीक्ष्णम् ॥ १३५ ॥

Stanza 135: If the Moon is aspected by the lord of the sign he occupies, he will have a sumptuous meal. Otherwise, the result will be contrary. If the Moon has Ithasala with Jupiter, he has a meal given to him with respect. If the Moon's Ithasala is with the Sun, he will have pure and holy food of hot taste.

शुक्रे सुस्वादुरसं सहास्यगीतं बुधे जनाकीर्णम् ।
शास्त्रकथाढचं शनिना कुस्थानगतं कुजे चोष्णम् ॥ १३६ ॥

Stanza 136: When the Moon has Ithasala with Venus, the meal is to the querent's desire. If the Moon's Ithasala is with Mercury, the querent will have excellent meals in a party, with music and entertainment. The Moon in Ithasala with Saturn or Mars denotes food in an out-of-the-way place or hot meals respectively.

यदि वदति भोजनार्थे निमन्त्रितो यामि ? शशिमहोसुतयो:
एकस्थितयो: केन्द्रे सुथशिलयोर्वाऽपि पूर्णता भवति ॥ १३७ ॥

Stanza 137: If the question is "will I attend the dinner invited for"; say that he will have a satisfactory dinner if the Moon and Mars are in conjunction in a Kendra or in mutual Ithasala.

विधिनाऽनेन शने: स्यात्कुभोजनं ज्ञसितयोरभीष्टान्नम् ।
जीवस्य तुष्टिजनकं होरेशे तनुखगे स्वयमुपैति ॥ १३८ ॥

Stanza 138: If Saturn is the planet, the food will be unattractive; if Mercury or Venus, the food will be to the entire satisfaction of the querent. If the ruler of the hora in which Jupiter is placed occupies the ascendant or the 10th, the querent without any effort on his part will be invited and served with food to his contentment.

NOTES

As in modern days, people in ancient times also were getting themselves invited for parties, dinners, etc., even though ordinarily either for want of an official position or status in the public they did not deserve such invitations. Stanzas 133 to 138 deal with the topic of getting such invitations and the type of food that would be served, etc. According to stanza 137, if Mars is in conjunction with the Moon in a Kendra or in Ithasala, the querent will not only be invited but would get good food. If Saturn is the planet involved, that is in conjunction with the Moon in a Kendra or in Ithasala with the Moon, the querent would get food he does not like. If Mercury or Venus is the planet in conjunction with the Moon in a Kendra or in Ithasala with the Moon, wholesome food will be served and the querent will derive complete satisfaction.

The second part of stanza 138 requires a little elucidation. Jupiter at the time of query is in some hora-the Sun or the Moon. If the lord of the hora occupies the ascendant or the 10th, the querent will be invited unasked and without effort on his part and served with food which is to his heart's content.

There is also a view that this hora refers to Kala Hora. Each day has 24 horas, the first hora commencing at sunrise and succeeding in a particular order.

Thus on Sunday the first hora is ruled by the Sun and the subsequent horas succeed in the order Venus, Mercury, Moon, Saturn, Jupiter, Mars, Sun, etc., until the first hora at sunrise on the morning of Monday will be ruled by the Moon. Suppose the query is at 3-30 p.m. on a Tuesday, and suppose the sunrise is at 6 a.m. between 3 and 4 p.m. on Tuesday, the hora is that of Venus. It would be more correct to say "if the lord of the hora, occupying the I or the X" instead of what is given in the stanza, viz., "if the lord of the hora occupied by Jupiter", etc. Planets as such cannot occupy horas as per hora division. If by hora is meant one of the sub-divisions, then only two horas are possible, viz., those of the Sun and the Moon and the stanza becomes clear. Suppose Jupiter occupies the Sun's hora: Then if the Sun is in the ascendant or the 10th, the result attributed to the combination will hold good. I think this latter interpretation is more sound.

यश्चन्द्रेण मुथशिली तस्मिन्त्रीशे तनोः स्वगृहभोज्यम् ।
वित्तेशे भृत्यगृहे भ्रातॄणां सहजपे तथाऽन्यत्र ॥ १३९ ॥

Stanza 139: The invitation for meals will be from the party signified by the house the lord of which happens to be in Ithasala. with the Moon. If he is lord of Lagna, the dinner will be in his own house; if of the 2nd, from employees; if of the 3rd, from brothers and so on.

NOTES

See the house the planet is in Ithasala with the Moon rules. The meals will be in the place appropriate to the house. Suppose; Jupiter is in Ithasala with the Moon and Jupiter happens to own the 5th house, then the invitation will come from children.

लग्नस्थिते सूर्यसुतेऽथ राहौ मूर्येक्षिते वैरिनिमन्त्रितस्य ।
स्याच्छत्रघातः शशिभौमयोश्च लग्नस्थयोः
सौरिदृशाऽस्ति घातः ॥ १४० ॥

Stanza 140: If Saturn or Rahu is in the ascendant aspected by the Sun, he will be invited by enemies and be attacked. If the Moon and Mars are in Lagna aspected by Saturn, the querent will be assaulted.

जीवे सिते लग्नगते बलाढ्ये चन्द्रे बुधे लग्नगते शुभान्विते ।
त्रिलाभषष्ठास्पदगैश्च पापैः स्यात्प्रेमनिर्वैरकरं
सुभोजनम् ॥ १४१ ॥

Stanza 141: He will be given agreeable meals by a friendly host if strong Jupiter and Venus, or strong Moon and Mercury are in the ascendant conjoined with benefics, and malefics occupy the 3rd, 6th, 10th and 11th.

भोज्यं बुभुक्षा भोक्ता च सुखाप्ताङ्गबलक्रमात् ।
लग्नपो भोज्यदस्तेषां बलेन फलमादिशेत् ॥ १४२ ॥

Stanza 142: The 4th house signifies the type of food, the 11th signifies hunger and the Lagna denotes the eater or Khadaka. The lord of Lagna is Bhojyadi. So the indications should be studied.

तुर्येशला भाधिपतीत्यशाले शुभग्रहेक्षायुतितः सुभोज्यम् ।
इत्थं खलग्नास्तपतीत्थशाले लाभेश्वरे तत्सुखलाभ
ऊह्यः ॥ १४३ ॥

Stanza 143: If the lords of the 4th and the 11th are in Ithasala and are aspected by benefics, he gets excellent meals. If the lord of the 11th is in Ithasala with the lord of the 10th, ascendant or the 7th, the querent happily enjoys the dinner.

On Dreams

लग्नेऽर्के नृपति वह्नि शस्त्रं पश्यति लोहितम् ।
श्वेतं पुष्पं सितं वस्त्रं गन्धे नारीं च शीतगौ ॥ १४४ ॥

Stanza 144: If the Sun occupies the ascendant, the querent sees in his dream a king, fire, weapon or a bloody act. If the Moon is in the ascendant, he will see in the dream white flower, white cloth scent, or a woman.

रक्तमांसप्रवालं च सुवर्ण धरणीसुते ।
बुधे खे गमनं जीवे धनं बन्धुसमागमम् ॥ १४५ ॥

Stanza 145: If Mars occupies the Lagna, the dream will be about blood, flesh, pearl or gold; if Mercury-journeying in the heavens; Jupiter-money and the visit of relatives.

जलावगाहनं शुक्रे शनौ तुङ्गावरोहणम् ।
लग्ने लग्नांशपवशात्स्वप्नो वाच्योऽथ वा बुधैः ॥ १४६ ॥

Stanza 146: If the ascendant is occupied by Venus, the dream will be about bathing, in a tank or river and if by Saturn, climbing elevated places such as hills, tall buildings, etc., or the nature of dream can be divined according to Navamsa Lagna.

सर्वोत्तमवलाद्वाऽपि खेटाद्बुद्ध्या विचिन्तयेत् ।
बलसाम्ये फलं मिश्रं दुःस्वप्नो निर्बलैः खगैः ॥ १४७ ॥

Stanza 147: Or the nature of the dream should be ascertained with reference to the strongest planet in the query chart. If the planetary influences are evenly disposed, the querent will have ordinary dreams. If all planets are weak, he will have evil dreams.

On Special Questions

NOTES

The combinations for getting good and evil dreams and what one will dream of are listed in stanzas 144 to 147. The planet in the ascendant, or the strongest planet in the horoscope or the lord of the Navamsa Lagna gives the clue for the dream one may have or one may have had. When these rules were framed, the importance attached to dreams was so great that many thought they should ascertain in advance what they will see in their dreams.

रविलग्ने शशिदृष्टे रविशशिसमेतलग्नद्वा ॥
स्वप्नं दुष्टं प्रवदेत्प्रष्टुर्लग्नान्तरात्कालः ॥ १४८ ॥

Stanza 148: If the Sun is in the ascendant aspected by the Moon or if both the Sun and the Moon are in the ascendant, the querent will have a bad dream; the duration of the dream corresponds to the duration of the rising sign at the time of query.

NOTES

This stanza has been taken from Bhattotpala.

On Sport

लग्नेशजामित्रपतीत्थशाले सुस्नेहदृष्ट्या त्वनयोर्द्वयोश्व ।
आखेटकः स्यात्सफलोऽरिदृष्ट्याचास्यान्निष्फलो
वाऽल्पफलोऽति कष्टात् ॥ १४९ ॥

Stanza 149: When the lords of the ascendant the 7th are in Ithasala and in mutual friendly aspect, one will have an enjoyable hunting expedition. If the aspect is inimical, the expedition will be difficult and a failure too.

लग्नेश्वरे द्यूनगते विलग्ने जायेश्वरे स्यान्मृगया प्रभूता ।
जामित्रनाथे हिबुके नभः स्थे चाखेटकः स्वल्पतरोऽपि
न स्यात् ॥ १५० ॥

Stanza 150: When the lord of the ascendant is in the 7th and vice versa, the hunting will be successful. If the lord of the 7th is in the 4th or 10th, it will not result in any catch.

ज्ञाभौमौ सबलौ सिद्धिरस्तांशे भृगयाच्युतिः ।
लग्नाद्द्यूने तत्पती च हेतुस्तैर्जलराशिगैः ॥ १५१ ॥

जलजं खेटकं ब्रूयाद्वन्यक्षैवन संभवः ।
क्रूराक्रान्तानि यावन्ति मध्ये भानीन्दुलग्नयोः ।
तावन्तः प्राणिनो वाच्या द्वित्रिघ्नाः स्वांशकादिषु ॥ १५२ ॥

Stanzas 151 and 152: If Mercury and Mars are strong, the catch will be good. If they are combust or in the 7th in the Navamsa, the querent has to abandon the 'hunting." The object of hunting is denoted by the lord of the 4th or the 10th occupying the 7th. If the Rasi happens to be watery, the catch in view are aquatic animals; if it is a Vana Rasi, the catch in view is wild animals. The querent will catch as many animals as the number of malefic planets intervening between the ascendant and the Moon. The number is to be doubled or trebled according as the malefics concerned are in their own navamsas or dwadasamsas.

NOTES

The four stanzas given above deal with success or failure in hunting expeditions, the nature and number of animals that will be caught, etc.

If the lord of the 4th or the 10th occupies the 7th, then note down the nature of the sign in the 7th-watery, quadrupedal, airy, etc., and accordingly say that the hunter's object is to catch fish, fowl or four-legged animals.

I do not think these combinations can have any relevancy to modern times.

All life is held in great sanctity by the Hindu sages and it passes one's comprehension why or how killing animals became a sport in this land. The combinations are given just because they are in the original work.

On Disputes

क्रूरः खचरो लग्ने विवादपृच्छासु जयति विवादे तम् ।
सर्वावस्थासु परं नीचेऽस्ते जयति न द्विषतः ॥ १५३ ॥

Stanza 153: When malefics are in the ascendant, the querent will win in the dispute. When the lord of the ascendant is debilitated or cambost, victory over the enemy is not possible.

लग्नद्यूने मुक्त्वा परस्परं क्रूरयोर्झंकटदृष्टौ ।
विवदद्द्वादियुग तच्छुरिकाभ्यां प्रहरति तदैवम् ॥ १५४ ॥

Sianza 154: If malefics posited in other houses than the ascendant and the 7th house are in mutual hostile aspect, the disputants will fight and assault each other.

NOTES

According to stanza 153, malefics in the ascendant favour the querent. The ascendant lord in debilitation or in combustion makes it difficult for the querent to win. As per stanza 154 if malefics present in any houses (except the ascendant and the 7th) are in mutual inimical aspect (i.e., opposition or square), the disputants will intensify the fight causing violence to each other.

Probably this 'assaulting' was necessary when enemies crossed their swords. But when applying to litigation, disputes, etc., we can say that the case will be fought to the bitter end.

लग्ने द्यूने च यदि क्रूरः खचरो विवादिनोर्न तदा
कलहनिवृत्तिः काले जयति हि बलवान् गतबलन्तु ॥ १५५ ॥

Stanza 155: If the ascendant and the 7th are occupied by malefics, there will be no peaceful end to the dispute. In due course the more powerful will vanquish his opponent.

NOTES

If malefics are situated in Lagna and the 7th, the more powerful of the two malefics indicate final success to the party signified. Thus if the malefic in the ascendant is more powerful, then the querent will succeed over his opponent.

लग्नेशसुतदः सौम्याःकेन्द्रे सन्धिर्न वाऽन्यथा ।
लग्नद्यूनेशषष्ठेशारित्वेऽप्यन्योन्यविग्रहः ॥ १५६ ॥

Stanza 156: If the lords of the ascendant and the 5th are in Kendras with benefics, there will be an agreement between the parties. Otherwise not. If the lords of the 6th and the 7th are inimical, mutual enmity will prevail.

NOTES

Lords of the ascendant and the 5th must be in quadrants conjoined by benefics to signify peace. If there is no such conjunction or if the conjunction is afflicted by malefic association or aspect, there will be no peace or understanding. The disputants will continue to be enemies if the lords of the 6th and the 7th are enemies.

The above four stanzas are from *Bhuvana Deepika*.

On The Traveller

गृहमागतो न यदसौ किं बद्धः किमथवा हतः ? इति प्रश्ने ।
मूर्तौ क्रूरो यदि तन्न हतो बद्धोऽथवा पुरुषः ॥ १५७ ॥

Stanza 157: If the question "will my man who has gone away return home or not, or is he in incarceration or killed" be put, say the person is neither killed nor imprisoned if malefics are in the ascendant.

त्रिकोणचतुरस्त्रास्तस्थितः पापग्रहो यदि ।
ग्रहैर्निरीक्षितः पापैर्नूनं बन्धनमादिशेत् ॥ १५८ ॥

Stanza 158: The person who has gone away is under restriction if malefics are in 4th, 5th, 7th, 8th and 9th aspected by malefics.

सप्तमगोऽष्टमगो वा चेत् क्रूरस्तद्धतेपि वा बद्धः ।
मूर्तौ च सप्तमे वा यद्वा लग्नेऽष्टमेऽपि भवेत् ।
क्रूरस्तदसौ पुरुषो बद्धश्च हतश्च मुच्यते च परम् ॥ १५९ ॥

Stanza 159: If malefics are in the 7th or the 8th, the fugitive will have been beaten and imprisoned. When malefics are in the ascendant, the 7th or the 8th, the fugitive will be imprisoned, beaten and then let off.

बद्धः सप्ताष्टमे क्रूरे मूर्त्यस्ते चाष्टलग्नगे ।
बद्धो विमुच्चतेत्याशु क्रूरः श्रेयांस्तनौ तदा ॥ १६० ॥

Stanza 160: When malefics are in the 7th and the 8th, or in the ascendant, and the 7th or the 8th and the 1st, the fugitive in imprisonment will be released quickly. When malefics are in Lagna, favourable results ensue.

NOTES

The above four stanzas are from *Bhuvana Deepika* and they give combinations for the imprisonment and release of the person who has gone to a distant place.

Release of the Imprisoned Traveller

बद्धोऽस्ति तत्किं भविते ति प्रश्ने विमुच्यतेऽसौ खलुमृत्युयोगे ।
कदा विमुच्येदिति पृच्छमाने शुभं कदा भावि च
तैर्मुंतिः स्यात् ॥ १६१ ॥

On Special Questions

Stanza 161:- The question "what will happen to the person in captivity? should be answered thus If there is a Mrityu Yoga as per judicial astrology, say he will be released. The answer to the question "when will he be released" is, he will die if there are malefic yogas.

NOTES

According to Natal Astrology, when there is a powerful Mrityu Yoga, the child dies quickly. If the same yoga is present in the Prasna chart and the Prasna is "what will happen to the person in imprisonment", the result is, he will be released from captivity. If other malefic yogas are present and the question is put as to "when he will be alright", malefic combinations cause death.

मुक्तिप्रश्ने यदा केन्द्रे केन्द्रेशाः स्युनं मोक्षदाः ।
तस्मिन्वर्षेऽथ लग्नेशः पतितः केन्द्रगेन च ॥ १६२ ॥

संबन्धेप्सुः स चेत्क्रूरो मृतीशः स्यात्तदा मृतिः ।
लग्नेशेऽस्तमितेऽम्बुस्थे कुजदृष्टे तदा मृतिः ॥ १६३ ॥

Stanzas 162 and 163: When the lords of Kendras are in Kendras, the imprisoned person will not be released. When the lord of the ascendant in the yearly chart is fallen and associated with a malefic occupying a Kendra and the lord of the 8th is a malefic planet, the fugitive will die. If the lord of the Lagna is combust, occupies the 4th and is aspected by Mars, the person dies.

NOTES

The person gone away will not be released if the Kendras are occupied by their lords. The prisoner will die if in the yearly chart (cast according to Tajaka principles—vide my book Varshaphal), the lord of the ascendant is "fallen", is debilitated and afflicted and has joined a malefic planet occupying a Kendra and the lord of the 8th is also a malefic.

To me, it occurs, there is no need to cast the yearly chart. If the Prasna chart has the afflictions mentioned in the above stanzas—debilitation of lord of Lagna, etc., the prisoner will die within a year. When Neelakanta says tasmin varshe, it implies the casting of the chart for the year in question.

चन्द्राश्राम्बुगपापेन मृत्युनाथेन योगकृत् ।
तदा गुप्त्यां मृतिश्चन्द्रः केन्द्रे मन्दयुगीक्षितः ॥ १६४ ॥

दीर्घपीडा च भौमेन युग्दृष्टे बन्धताडने ।
दृश्यार्धे लग्नपश्चेत्स्याद्व्ययपेनेत्थशालवान् ॥ १६५ ॥

पलायते तदा बद्धों व्ययगे लग्नगेऽपि वा ।
तृतीयनवमस्वामी व्ययगो लग्नपेन च ॥ १६६ ॥

यदीत्थशालयोगेऽप्सुस्तदाऽपि च पलायते ।
दृश्यार्धेह्यपचारेण चन्द्रो मुथशिलो तदा ॥ १६७ ॥

बन्धमोक्षस्त्रिधर्मेशः सद्ग्रहः शीघ्रमोक्षकृत् ।
पतितेन्दुस्त्रिधर्मस्थग्रहसम्बन्धकृत्तदा ॥ १६८ ॥

केन्द्रस्थत्रिभवेशेन योगेप्सुश्चेत्तदाऽचिरात् ।
यावच्छुको बली लग्ने तावत्कर्त्ता बलाधिकः ॥ १६९ ॥

अस्तंगते शनौ शुक्रे बद्धमोक्षादिसम्भवः ।
म्रियते येन योगेन तेन योगेन मुच्यते ॥ १७० ॥

मेषे तुले च शीघ्रं स्यात्कर्के नक्र सकष्टता ।
स्थिरेऽचिराद्द्विदेहस्थे मोक्षो मध्यमकालतः ॥ १७१ ॥

Stanzas 164 to 171: If the Moon is in association with a malefic occupying the 4th or is with the lord of the 8th, the person will die in prison. If the Moon occupying a Kendra is associated with or aspected by Saturn, he will have long suffering; if aspected by or conjoined with Mars, he will be beaten in the cell. If the lord of the Lagna is in Drisyardha having Ithasala with the lord of the 12th, the person will escape from the prison. If the lord of the 12th is in the 1st and the lords of the 3rd and the 12th are in the 12th in Ithasala with the lord of the 1st, then also the fugitive will escape from prison. If the Moon occupying Drisyardha has Muthasila with any planet, the prisoner will be released. He will get his freedom early if the lords of the 3rd and the 9th are benefics. If the afflicted Moon has Ithasala with a planet situated in the 3rd or the 9th, then also he will be discharged. When the Moon has Ithasala with the lord of the 3rd or the 9th occupying a Kendra, there will be early release. As long as a strong Venus is in Lagna, the authority will be able to hold the person in custody. If Saturn or Venus is in combustion, the chances for slipping out will be bright. The combination for death in a birth chart, if present in Prasna chart, indicates release from prison. If Saturn or Mars is in Aries or Libra, the release will be early. If they are in Cancer or Capricorn, release will be secured after much difficulty. If they are in fixed signs, the release comes late. If they are in common signs, the time of release will neither be early nor late.

NOTES

The above eight stanzas give combinations for the non-release, release, escape, etc., of the man in custody. In stanza 166, the statement "so long as Venus is strong in Lagna" should be understood thus: At the time of query Venus is strongly placed in the ascendant. Then the authority will be strong enough to hold the person in detention. But after Venus leaves the sign by transit, the authority will become weak and the prisoner may opt for freedom.

According to stanza 170, if supposing a yoga or combination that usually denotes death when applied to birth horoscope is present in the Prasna chart, then you can declare that the person will be released.

The other combinations are simple and can be easily understood.

By *drisyardha* referred to in stanzas 165 and 167 is meant the visible heavens which means the six houses from Lagna to the 7th house via the 10th, *i.e.* the Lagna, 12th, 11th, 10th, 9th and 8th houses.

Queries Bearing on Ships, etc.

क्षेमायतं वहिनस्य मज्जनं वपनं जले ।
पण्यव्यवहृतौ लाभो वाऽपि प्रश्नचतुष्टयम् ॥ १७२ ॥

Stanza 172: There are four questions pertaining to ships, safe voyage, difficulties on the sea, breaking-up on the sea and gain or loss in its sale.

नौर्लाभदा स्यान्मम नेति पृष्टे केन्द्रे शुभाश्चेदितरेषु पापाः ।
बलोज्झिताः क्षेमजयार्थदा नौर्भावीति वाच्यं विदुषा
विमृश्य ॥ १७३ ॥

Stanza 173: If "will I profit from the ship" is the question, say that it brings gain and benefit to the querent if benefics are in quadrants and malefics are weak and occupy the 3rd, 6th or 11th houses.

लग्राधिपे वक्रिणि चांशनाथे व्यावृत्य नौरेति च मार्गतः सा ।
चेत्सौम्यदृष्टः कुशलेन पापैदृष्टस्तदा वस्तु विनेति
वाच्यम् ॥ १७४ ॥

Stanza 174: If the lords of Lagna and Navamsa Lagna are retrograde and aspected by benefics, the ship with merchandise arrives safe. If the lords of Lagna and Navamsa Lagna are aspected by malefics, the ship arrives without any merchandise.

विलग्नरन्ध्राधिपती स्वगेहे प्रवेक्ष्यतश्चद्व्यवहारलाभः ।
यदाऽटमे सौम्यखगा बलाढ्यास्तदा तरी लाभसुखप्रदा
स्यात् ॥ १७५ ॥

Stanza 175: If the lords of Lagna and the 8th are in their respective signs, gain will accrue in the transaction. A strong benefic in the 8th indicates gain and other beneficial results.

कुशलाऽऽयाति पृच्छायां मृत्युयोगे सनागते ।
तदा नौरेति शीघ्रेण लाभाद्यां चान्ययोगतः ॥ १७६ ॥

Stanza 176: If "will the ship arrive safe" is the query, say it will arrive early if Mrityu Yoga is present in the chart. But for predicting benefits other combinations are to be looked into.

लग्नेशं चन्द्रनाथं वा चन्द्रं वा मृत्युपो यदि ।
पश्येत्क्रूरदृशा नावा समं श्यति नौपतिः ॥ १७७ ॥

Stanza 177: If the lord of the 8th is in an inimical aspect with the lord of the ascendant or the lord of the sign held by the Moon or the Moon himself, the owner (commander) of the ship will get drowned in the sea.

लग्नेशोऽष्टपतिः स्वस्वगेहं नालोकते यदि ।
तदा यानेऽस्य वक्तव्यं निश्चितं मज्जनं बुधैः ॥ १७८ ॥

Stanza 178: If the lords of the ascendant and the 8th do not aspect their respective houses, it is certain that the ship in voyage will get sunk.

तावुभौ सप्तमस्थौ चेज्जले बापनिकां वदेत् ।
द्यूने वापनिकां कृत्वा यानमायाति मन्दिरम् ॥ १७९ ॥

Stanza 179: If the lords of the ascendant or the 8th are in the 7th, the merchandise will be lost but the ship will return home safe.

लग्नचन्द्रपती क्रूरदृष्ट्याऽन्योन्यं यदीक्षितौ ।
तदा पोतजनानां च मिथः कलहमादिशेत् ॥ १८० ॥

Stanza 180: If there is mutual hostile aspect between the lords of Lagna and Chandra Lagna, the men on ship will be involved in mutual quarrels.

Truth of Rumours

लग्ननं तु लग्नेश्वरशीतगूदयैः शुभान्वितैः केन्द्रगतैस्तु सत्या ।
शुभदृग्योगतः सौम्यां वार्ता सत्यां विनिर्दिशेत् ॥ १८१ ॥

Stanza 181: If the ascendant, the ascendant lord and the Moon are conjoined with or aspected by benefics or occupy a Kendra, favourable news received about the ship will be reliable.

पापदृग्योगतो दुष्टा वार्ता सत्येति कीर्यते ।
लग्नेश्वरे भाविवक्रं मिथ्या वार्ता भविष्यति ॥ १८२ ॥

Stanza 182: If the above factors are afflicted, evil news about the ship will be correct. If the ascendant lord is retrograde, then the news, whether good or bad, will be unreliable.

On Purchase And Sale

क्रेता लग्नपतिर्ज्ञेयो विक्रेताऽग्रपतिः स्मृतः ।
गृह्णाम्यहमिदं वस्तु प्रश्न एवंविधे सति ॥ १८३ ॥

Stanza 183: To answer the question "Can I purchase this article", consider the lord of the ascendant as the purchaser and lord of the 2nd or lord of the 11th as the indicator of sale.

बलशाली विलग्नं चेद्गृह्यते तत्क्रयाणकम् ।
तस्मात्क्रयणकाल्लाभः प्रष्टुर्भवति निश्चितम् ॥ १८४ ॥

Stanza 184: If the ascendant is strongly disposed, the article can be purchased as it will be definitely gainful to the querent.

विक्रीणाम्यमुक वस्तु प्रश्न एवंविधे सति ।
आयस्थाने बलवति विक्रेतव्यं क्रयाणकम् ॥ १८५ ॥

Stanza 185: If the question is "shall I sell the article", say that it can be sold for profit if the 11th house is occupied by powerful planets.

NOTES

Stanzas 183 to 185 will be found to be very useful in the daily lives of businessmen, merchants and even common people for buying and selling articles.

The questions are: (a) Can I purchase this article? (b) Can I sell this article?.

The idea of purchasing an article is to sell it for a profit and the object of selling an article is to get profit. The Lagna lord represents the purchase, while the lord of the 2nd or the 11th is the significator of the sale. It will be to the advantage of the querent to purchase the article if the ascendant and its lord are strongly disposed.

The querent will get good profit when the 11th house is strongly disposed, i.e., occupied by powerful planets.

The word "Agrapathi" is translated by commentators as lord of the 10th while some say it means either the lord of the 2nd or the 11th. If the former meaning is accepted, then as per stanza 183, the lord of the 10th becomes the indicator of contemplated sale.

We have dealt with hundreds of questions under this category. When the lords of the ascendant and the 11th are in mutual trines or sextiles, one can easily purchase the article in view. Then combination has to be slightly varied by our intelligence according to the nature of the 'article' involved. If it is house or landed property, Mars should not be afflicted. If it is a business concern, Mercury should not be afflicted. If it is a factory, Saturn should not be afflicted. An astrologer can clearly advise his client on the basis of the three stanzas given above subject to his own intelligent interpretation.

On Crops

दिशि कस्यां भवेत्सस्यनिष्पत्ति: क्व सा नहि ।
पूर्वे देशस्य भङ्गो हि क्व दिशि क्वतमे नहि ॥ १८६॥

Stanza 186: To answer the question, "In which direction do the crops thrive; in which direction they do not thrive well", first of all ascertain which part of the land will be afflicted.

चतुर्णामपि केन्द्राणां मध्ये यत्र शुभग्रह: ।
तस्यां च सस्यनिष्पत्ति: स्वस्थं चैव भविष्यति ॥ १८७ ॥

Stanza 187: The crops will thrive well in the direction signified by the Kendra which is occupied by benefic planets.

यस्यां दिशि शनि: पापैर्यूतो वाऽप्यवलोकित: ।
दिशि तस्यां च तत्स्वास्थ्यं दुर्भिक्षं च भविष्यति ॥ १८८ ॥

Stanza 188: The land in the direction indicated by the Kendra which is afflicted by Saturn and other malefic planets will be unsuitable and as a consequence famine will result.

दिशि यस्यां रविस्तत्र धान्यनाशो नृपाद्भवेत् ।
यत्रापि मङ्गलस्तत्र धान्यमाशोऽग्निभीस्तथा ॥ १८९ ॥

Stanza 189: The direction signified by the Sun is exposed to the danger of destruction of the crops by the king. In the direction signified by Mars, the crop will be destroyed by fire.

यस्यां दिशि शुभा: खेटा: समस्तबलशालिन: ।
निष्पन्ना सैव विज्ञेया सस्यस्वास्थ्यं च तत्र हि ॥ १९० ॥

Stanza 190: The crops will flourish well in the direction signified by the Kendra occupied by fortified benefic planets.

केन्द्रेषु सर्वतः पापाः समस्तबलसंयुताः ।
देशस्तदा विनष्टोऽसौ ज्ञातव्यः शास्त्रकोविदैः ॥ १९१ ॥

Stanza 191: Astrologers should know that if all the Kendras are occupied by powerful malefics, the entire land will be unfit for cultivation.

NOTES

Though these questions used to be put by big landlords possessing vast estates or rulers of principalities, the principles can be made applicable to modern times also for predicting how crops say in a state or in a part of the country thrive. Of course in peace times there are no depredations of rulers, but destruction can be wrought by agitators, by way of incendiarism or other modes of destruction.

Chapter 4
Miscellaneous Matters

लग्नपो मृत्युपश्चापि मृत्यौ स्यातामुभौ यदि ।
स्थितौ द्रेष्काण एकस्मिन्प्रष्टुर्लाभस्तदा ध्रुवम् ॥ १ ॥

Stanza 1: The querent is sure to gain if the lords of the ascendant and the 8th are in the same Drekkana.

एवं द्वादशभावेषु द्रेष्काणैरेव केवलम् ।
बुधो विनिश्चयं ब्रूयाद्योगेश्चन्येषु निःस्पृहः ॥ २ ॥

Stanza 2: In this manner, by considering the Drekkanas should the discerning astrologer infer the results in respect of all the houses even by not taking into account other combinations.

प्रश्नकाले सौम्यवर्गे लग्ने यदधिको भवेत् ।
ग्रहभावानपेक्षेण तदाऽऽख्येयं शुभं फलम् ॥ ३ ॥

Stanza 3: The Bhavas ruled by planets having a larger share of benefic vargas in Prasna Lagna will show auspicious results.

NOTES

Stanzas 1 and 2 give general combinations. If the lords of the ascendant and a Bhava are in conjunction in the Bhava in the same Drekkana, the events of the Bhava will thrive well.

According to stanza 3, suppose the Lagna at the time of query is Virgo 5°. Find out shodasavargas of Lagna. Suppose Jupiter gets the largest share of vargas. Jupiter rules the 4th and 7th houses. Then the events of these two houses thrive well.

लग्नाधिपश्च लाभस्याधीशश्च दायको भवेत् ।
लग्नाधिपस्य योगो लाभाधिशेन लाभकरः ॥ ४ ॥

Stanza 4: The benefit-giving planets are the lords of the ascendant and the 11th. It should be noted that a combination of the lords of the ascendant and the 11th is always beneficial and confers good results.

भवति परमलाभकरस्तदैव स यदि चन्द्रदृग्लाभे ।
योगाः सर्वेऽन्यफलाश्चन्द्रमृते व्यक्तमेतच्च ॥ ५ ॥

Stanza 5: The beneficial capacity of the lords of the ascendant and the 11th becomes intensified if they have the aspect of the Moon. It is clear that in the absence of the Moon's aspect, the potential of any Yoga is reduced.

कर्माधीशेन नवमं कर्माधीशेन च निवृत्त्यधीशेन ।
मृत्युपतिना च योगे लाभाधीशस्य वक्तव्यम् ॥ ६ ॥

Stanza 6: There will be immense gain if the 9th is aspected by or conjoined with the lord of the 10th; or if the lord of the 11th is joined by the lord of the 10th, the 12th or the 8th.

तत्तत्स्थानेक्षणतः पुण्यविवृद्धिश्च कर्मवृद्धिश्च ।
विबुधैस्तदा निवृत्तिर्मृत्युर्भावा परेऽप्येवम् ॥ ७ ॥

Stanza 7: If the 8th and 12th houses are aspected by benefics, there will be increase of righteousness and good actions. Other Bhavas should also be studied likewise.

लग्नेशो यदि षष्ठः स्वयमेत्य रिपुर्भवत्यात्मा ।
मृत्युदष्टमगोऽसौ व्ययगोऽसौ सततं व्ययं कुरुते ॥ ८ ॥

Stanza 8: When the lord of Lagna is in the 6th, the querent's own Atma will be his enemy. When the ascendant lord is in the 8th, death will ensue. When the lord of Lagna is in the 12th, the querent will always have losses.

लग्नस्थं चन्द्रजं चन्द्रः क्रूरो वा यदि पश्यति ।
धनलाभो भवत्याशु कित्वनर्थोऽपि पृच्छतः ॥ ९ ॥

Stanza 9: When Mercury occupying the ascendant is aspected by the Moon or other malefics, there will be early gain of money. But the querent will also have troubles.

General Judgment of Houses

इन्दुः सर्वत्र बीजाभो लग्नं च कुसुमप्रभम् ।
फलेन सदृशोंऽशश्च भावः स्वादुसमप्रभः ॥ १० ॥

Stanza 10: The Moon is always to be considered as the seed, the ascendant as the flower, the navamsa ascendant as the fruit and the house as taste.

लग्नपतिर्यदि लग्नं कार्याधीशश्च वीक्षते कार्यम् ।
लग्नाधीशः कार्ये कार्येशः पश्यति विलग्नम् ॥ ११ ॥

लग्नेशः कार्येशं विलोकयेल्लग्नपं च कार्येशः ।
शीतगुदृष्टौ सत्यां परिपूर्णा कार्यसंसिद्धिः ॥ १२ ॥

Stanzas 11 and 12: If the lord of the ascendant aspects the ascendant and the significator aspects the house; or if the ascendant lord aspects the house and the significator aspects the ascendant; or if the ascendant lord aspects the significator and the significator aspects the ascendant lord. In all these cases, the object will be completely fulfilled if there is the Moon's aspect also.

NOTES

The significator is the planet owning the house of an event. Thus, if the question is about marriage, the significator is the lord of the 7th; if the query is about issues, the significator is the lord of the 5th; if the query is about profession, the significator is the lord of the 10th. And the house referred to in the above two stanzas is the appropriate Bhava.

Thus for example, a query relates to a marriage and the ascendant is Leo. Then the factors involved will be the ascendant (Leo), its lord (the Sun), the 7th house (Aquarius) and its lord (Saturn).

If the Sun aspects the ascendant and Saturn aspects the 7th; or if the Sun aspects the 7th house and Saturn aspects the ascendant; or if the Sun aspects Saturn and Saturn aspects the Sun, the object of the query, *viz.*, marriage will be definitely fulfilled, provided the Moon also aspects either of the factors of the combination.

कथयन्ति पादयोगं पश्यति सौम्यो न यलग्नम् ।
लग्नाधिपं च पश्यति शुभग्रहश्चार्धयोगोऽत्र ॥ १३॥

एक: शुभ ग्रहो यदि पश्यति लग्नाधिपौ विलोकयति ।
पादोनयोगमाहुस्तदा बुधा: कार्यसंसिद्धि: ॥१४॥

Stanzas 13 and 14: If the Lagna is not aspected by a benefic, the benefic effect is one-fourth. When a benefic aspects the lord of the ascendant, the benefic effect is one-half. When a benefic aspects the ascendant, the good effect is three-fourths which means the object will be fulfilled.

NOTES

In the matter of judging an event, the strong disposition of the ascendant and its lord are essential. When a benefic planet aspects the ascendant, the benefic outcome will be 75% and consequently we may declare success. When only the lord is aspected by a benefic, the good effect is only 50% which means the chances of success are even. When there is no aspect on the Lagna, the result is not favourable.

On The Time Factor

उदयोपगतं राशिं तत्र कलोकृत्य लिप्तिका गुणयेत् ।
छायाङ्गुलैश्च कुर्यात् हृत्वा मुनिभिस्ततः शेषम् ॥ १५ ॥

ग्रहगुणकारो ज्ञेयो दैवविदा पञ्च विंशतिः सैका ।
मनवोऽङ्काऽष्टौ त्रितयं भवाश्च ५।२९।९४।९१८।३।११
सूर्यादितो ज्ञेयाः ॥ १६ ॥

गुणयित्वैवं प्राग्वत् हृत्वा सौम्यस्य यदि भवेदुदयः ।
कार्यप्राप्तिः प्रष्टुर्वक्तव्या नेतरैर्ग्रहैर्भवति ॥ १७ ॥

गुणकारैक्यविभक्तः कार्यः सूर्यादिगुणकसंशुद्धः ।
यस्य न शुद्ध्यति वर्गो विज्ञेयस्तद्दशात्कालः ॥ १८ ॥

आरदिवाकरशेषे दिवसाः पक्षाश्च भृगुशशिनोः ।
गुर्ववशेषे मासा ऋतवः सौम्ये शनैश्चरेऽब्दाः स्युः ॥ १९ ॥

Stanzas 15 to 19: Reduce the longitude of the ascendant (beginning from Aries) into minutes. It is called Kalapinda. Multiply this by the equinoctial shadow at the moment of query. Divide this product by 7. Reject the quotient. The remainder represents the planets (in the order the Sun—1, the Moon—2, Mars—3, Mercury—4, Jupiter—5, Venus—6 and Saturn—7) which is to be taken. Multiply again the Kalapinda by the concerned planetary factor; (the Sun—5, the Moon—21, Mars—14, Mercury—9, Jupiter—8, Venus and Saturn—11). Divide the product by the sum of the Gunakas from the Sun to the planet in question. Deduct from this remainder (y) the Gunaka of the Sun, etc. Whichever planet's Gunaka is not deductible should be considered the rising planet. If this planet is a benefic, the object of the query will be fulfilled. The time of fructification is indicated by the remainder y. If the rising planet is the Sun or Mars, the remainder (y) represents so many days. If it is Vênus or the Moon, the number represents the fortnight. If it is Jupiter, the number represents month, if Mercury—half-year and if Saturn, years.

NOTES

Stanzas 115 to 119 require some explanation though their practical application in modern times is doubtful, because equinoctial shadows cannot be measured during nights or when the days are cloudy, etc.

Suppose the ascendant at the time of query is Taurus 5° 54' and the length of the equinoctial shadow is 8.

First Process

Reducing the ascendant (Taurus 5° 54') to minutes we get 35° 54' = 2154', and this is Kalapinda. Multiply this by 8: 2154 × 8 = 17232. Dividing this by 7 (17232 ÷ 7 = 2461 5/7) we get 5 as remainder. Call this X. 5 represents Jupiter. The Gunaka or multiplying factor of Jupiter is 8.

Second Process

Multiplying the Kalapinda by 8 (multiplicator of Jupiter), we get 2154 × 8 = 17232. Dividing this product by the sum of the Gunakas (from the Sun to Jupiter), *viz.*, 57 (17232 ÷ 57 = 302 − 18/57), we get the remainder (y) as 18.

Third Process

Remainder	18
Deduct Sun's Gunaka	5
	13
Deduct Moon's Gunaka	21

So we get 13 points having passed in the Moon's Gunaka. The Moon is the rising planet and since the Moon is a benefic, the object of the query will be fulfilled. The Moon represents fortnight and here the realisation will be within 15 days.

As the equinoctial shadow cannot be measured at all times, this tedious method is not of much practical value.

आधानेऽथ प्राप्तौ गमनागमने पराजये विजये ।
रिपुनाशे वा काले पृच्छायां निश्चितं ब्रूयात् ॥ २० ॥

Stanza 20: In respect of questions bearing on conception, gain of money, arrival and departure, success or failure, and destruction of enemies, the above method of ascertaining the time of fructification can be successfully employed.

अकचटतपयशवर्गी रविकुजसितसौम्यजोवसौराणाम् ।
चन्द्रस्य च निर्दिष्टास्तैः स्युः प्रथमोद्धवैर्वर्णैः ॥ २१ ॥

ज्ञात्वा तस्माल्लग्नं विज्ञाय शुभाशुभं च वदेत् ।
वर्गादिमध्यमान्त्यैर्वर्णैः प्रश्नोद्धवैविषमराशिः ॥ २२ ॥

रात्रौ लग्नं प्रवदेत्पृच्छायुग्मं कुजज्ञजीवानाम् ।
सितरविजयोश्च नैवं रविशशिनोरेकराशित्वात् ॥ २३ ॥

तस्मात्प्रागवत्प्रवदेत्पृच्छासमये शुभाशुभं सर्वम् ।
कालस्य च विज्ञानादेतच्चिन्त्यं बहुप्रश्ने ॥ २४ ॥

Stanzas 21 to 24: The Sun, Mars, Venus, Mercury, Jupiter, Saturn and the Moon represent respectively the groups of letters commencing from *a, ka, cha, ta, tha, pa, ya,* and *sa*. On the basis of the first letter or syllable uttered by a querent the Lagna at night should be found and good and bad predicted. If the first letter is the 1st, 3rd, etc., in the group, then the Lagna is an odd sign. If it is 2nd or 4th in the group, it is an even sign.

As the Sun and the Moon have only one Rasi each, the question of an odd or even Rasi does not arise. Hence one should predict as before on the basis of the ascendant. This is the method used for deciding Lagnas where more than one query is put.

NOTES

The above stanzas require some explanation. The Sanskrit alphabet has 56 letters and these have been divided into seven groups, each group represented by a planet as follows :-

Planet	Varga letters commencing from							
Sun	अ	आ	इ	ई	उ	ऊ	ऋ	ॠ
	a	aa	i	ee	u	oo	ri	rii
	लृ	लॄ	ए	ऐ	ओ	औ		
	lu	loo	e	ai	o	ow		
Mars	क	ख	ग	घ	ङ			
	k	kha	ga	gha	gna			
Venus	च	छ	ज	झ	ञ			
	cha	chha	ja	jha	nya			
Mercury	ट	ठ	ड	ढ	ण			
	ta	tta	da	dha	na			
Jupiter	त	थ	द	ध	न			
	tha	thha	dha	ddha	na			
Saturn	प	फ	ब	भ	म			
	pa	pha	ba	bha	ma			
Moon	य	र	ल	व	श	ष		
	ya	ra	la	va	sa	sha		
	स	ह	ळ					
	sa	ha	la					

Suppose the letter uttered by the querent is Ma. Then the ruler is Saturn and the rising sign should be taken as Capricorn or Aquarius. Since Ma is an odd letter, the ascendant is aquarius.

When the first letter uttered by a querent comes under a benefic planet, good can be predicted. If it comes under a malefic planet, unfavourable results should be anticipated. By deciding the Lagna on the basis of the first letter and placing the planets as on that day, the Prasna chart can be answered as an Aroodha.

One's Own Thinking

स्वांशं विलग्ने यदि वा त्रिकोणे स्वांशे स्थितः पश्यति
धातुचिन्ताम् ।
परांशकस्थश्च करोति जीवं मूलं परंशोपगतः परांशम् ॥ २५ ॥

Stanza 25: If a planet occupying his own Navamsa aspects his own Navamsa in the Lagna, the 5th or the 9th, then the query refers to Dhatu. If the aspecting planet occupies the Navamsa of another planet, the query relates to Jeeva. If the aspecting planet occupies another planet's Navamsa and aspects another Navamsa in the Lagna, the query relates to Jeeva.

NOTES

This and the next stanza are from *Shatpanchasika*. As Prof. Rao observes in his English translation of this great work "the brevity and suggestiveness of Sanskrit words cannot be easily rendered into English" and stanza 25 is suggestive and concise.

One has to say to which a query refers—Dhatu (mineral), or Jeeva (animal) or Moola (vegetable). And the following combinations give the clue.

(a) A planet occupying his 'own Navamsa aspects Navamsa Lagna which should be owned by the planet: or the planet (occupying his own Navamsa) should aspect his own Navamsa in the 5th or 9th house. Under this combination, the query may be said to refer to Dhatu or mineral.

Suppose at the time of query, the ascendant is 24° Aries, the V house is 22° Leo and the 9th house 36° Sagittarius and Mars occupies Leo 3°. In the Navamsa chart I Mars is in Aries, the ascendant is Scorpio. (a) Mars occupying his own Navamsa aspects Navamsa Lagna which is also owned by Mars. The query (say about a missing article) refers to Dhatu or mineral. (b) A planet occupying not his own navamsa aspects his own Navamsa in the Lagna or in the 5th. or 9th house. Then the object relates to a living being or Jeeva. (c) A planet not occupying his own Navamsa and aspects another planet's (and not his own) Navamsa in Lagna or the 5th or 9th, the object relates to Moola or vegetable.

Example for (a)

	Mars		
	Navamsa I		
IX	Lagna	V	

Example for (b)

Lagna Leo 26°, Jupiter Libra 28°, V house Sagittarius 27°

			Jupiter
	Navamsa II		
V	Lagna		

Jupiter not occupying his own Navamsa aspects his own Navamsa in the 5th house. Hence the object of the query refers to a Jeeva.

Example for (c)

Saturn Libra 19°, I House Aries 23° IX House Sagittarius 27°

Saturn			
	Navamsa II		
IX		Lagna	

Saturn not occupying his own Navamsa aspects the Navamsa of the 9th house. The object refers to a Moola or vegetable kind.

धातुं मूलं जीवमित्योजराशौ युग्मे विन्द्यादेतदेव प्रतीपम् ।
लग्ने योंऽशस्तत्क्रमाद्गण्यमेवं संक्षेपोऽयं
                                    विस्तारात्ततप्रभेद ॥ २६ ॥

Stanza 26: In odd signs, the nine navamsas represent in regular order, Dhatu, Moola and Jeeva. In even signs, the order is reversed, the nature of the object should be ascertained on the basis of the rising navamsa. The rules given here are only brief. Details can be obtained from other sources.

NOTES

In odd signs (Aries, Gemini, Leo, etc.) the 1st, 4th and 7th Navamsas refer to Dhatu, the 2nd, 5th and 8th refer to Moola and the 3rd, 6th and 9th refer to Jeeva. In even signs (Taurus, Cancer, Virgo, etc.) the 1st, 4th and 7th refer to Jeeva, the 2nd, 5th and 8th to Moola and the 3rd, 6th and 9th to Dhatu.

बलिनौ केन्द्रोपतौ रवभौमौ धातुकरौ प्रश्ने ।
बुधसौरि मूलकरौ शशिगुरुशुक्राः स्मृता जीवाः ॥ २७ ॥

Stanza 27: If the Sun and Mars are fortified in a quadrant, the query will be about a Dhatu or mineral. If Mercury and Saturn are strongly placed in a kendra, the question relates to a Moola (vegetable). And if the Moon, Jupiter and Venus are strongly disposed in a kendra, the query will bear on a Jeeva or animal.

मेषासिंहलग्ने कुजार्कयुक्ते निरीक्षितेऽप्यथवा ।
धातोश्नन्तां प्रवदेद्युगघटकन्यागतैर्लग्नैः ॥ २८ ॥

बुधरविजयुतैर्मूलं वृषतुलहरिमीनचापकर्कटकैः ।
चन्द्रगुरुशुक्रयुक्तैर्दृष्टैर्जीवो विनिर्देश्यः ॥ २९ ॥

Stanzas 28 and 29: If the Ascendant is Aries, Scorpio or Leo and is occupied or aspected by the Sun and Mars, the query relates to a Dhatu. If the ascendant is Gemini, Aquarius or Virgo occupied or aspected by Saturn and Mercury, the query is about Moola. If the ascendant is Taurus, Leo, Pisces, Sagittarius or Cancer occupied or aspected by the Moon, Jupiter and Venus, the query is about Jeeva.

NOTES

The above three stanzas are from Utpala and they are clear.

लग्नलाभपयो: प्राणितयोर्यद्धावग: शशी ।
तस्य भावस्य या चिन्ता प्रष्टु: सा हृदि वर्तते ॥ ३० ॥

Stanza 30: The house occupied by the strong lords of the ascendant and the 11th in conjunction with the Moon reveals the nature of the query in the mind of the consultant.

एवं बलाधिकाच्चन्द्राल्लग्ननातो यत: स्थित: ।
दैवज्ञेन विनिर्णेय: प्रश्नसद्धावसम्भव: ॥ ३१ ॥

Stanza 31: In a similar manner, the astrologer can ascertain the nature of the query from the house in which the lord of the ascendant and powerful Moon are in conjunction.

NOTES

According to stanza 30, the lords of the ascendant and the 11th should be strongly disposed; whereas according to stanza 31, the Moon should be strong.

Miscellaneous Matters

Suppose either as per stanza 30 or 31, the conjunction of the strong Lagna and 11th lords and the Moon, the lord of Lagna and the strong Moon are in the 7th house. It is clear the question relates to the wife or partner. If the conjunction is in the 2nd it relates to finance. Similarly, the event signified by the Bhava in which the conjunction occurs will be uppermost in the mind of the querent.

आत्मसमं लग्नगतैस्तृतीयगैर्भ्रातरः सुतं सुतगैः ।
माता वा भगिनी वा शत्रुगतैः शत्रुभार्या स्यात् ॥ ३२ ॥

सप्तमसंस्थैर्नवमैर्धर्माश्रितयुग्गुरुर्दशमैः ।
स्वांशपतिमित्रशत्रुषु तथैव वाच्यं बलयुतेषु ॥ ३३ ॥

Stanzas 32 and 33: The question will be about a person who is closely connected with the querent if a planet is strongly placed in the ascendant; if in the 3rd, the query will be about brothers; if in the 5th about children; if in the 4th about mother or wife; if in the 6th about the enemy; if in the 7th about wife; if in the 9th about righteous people; if in the 10th, about preceptor. The prediction must also be made taking into due consideration whether the lord of the Navamsa Lagna is endowed with strength and is friendly or inimical to the lord of the ascendant.

NOTES

If the query "who is the person I am thinking about" is put, then it can be answered on the basis of stanzas 32 and 33. The house occupied by a planet endowed with strength gives the clue to the person the querent has in mind; and if such a house is the 3rd, it is about brothers; if it is the 6th, it is about enemies, etc. When more than one planet occupies a house or when more than one house is occupied by planets, the astrologer should carefully discern the strongest house and then give his finding.

If the lord of Navamsa Lagna occupies the Lagna, then the query will be about the querent himself. If the lord of the Navamsa Lagna is a friend of the lord of Lagna, the query is about a friend. If the Navamsa Lagna lord is an enemy of the Lagna lord, then the query is about the querent's enemy.

चरलग्ने चरभागे मध्याद्मृष्टे प्रवासचिन्ता स्यात् ।
भ्रष्टः सप्तमभवनात्पुनर्निवृत्तो यदि न वक्रो ॥ ३४ ॥

Stanza 34: If the ascendant is a movable sign and the rising Navamsa also being movable is the 6th, 7th, 8th or 9th, the query will be about a person who has gone to a far-off place. If the planet that has fallen' from the 7th is not retrograde, the person gone abroad will return. If the planet is retrograde, the person will not return.

NOTES

Stanzas 31 to 34 are again from *Shatpanchasika*. According to stanza 34, the query relates to one who may have gone to a foreign country if the Lagna and the Navamsa Lagna are both movable and the Navamsa Lagna happens also to be the 6th, 7th, 8th or 9th Navamsa. If suppose the Lagna is Cancer, then the 7th Navamsa answers the requirement. viz., the Navamsa should be movable and past the 5th.

Suppose at the time of query, a planet is in the 6th house just free from retrogression, the traveller will return. If the planet is retrograde, he will not return.

On Sexual Matters

अस्ते रविसितवक्रैः परजायां स्वां गुरौ बुधे वेश्याम् ।
जन्द्रे च वयः शशिवत् प्रवदेत्सौरेऽन्त्यजादीनाम् ॥ ३५ ॥

कुमारिकां बालशशी बुधश्व वृद्धां शनिः सूर्यगुरू प्रसूताम् ।
स्त्री कर्कशां भौमसितौ च धत्ते एवं वयः स्यात्पुरुषेषु
चैवम् ॥ ३६ ॥

Stanzas 35 and 36: Mars, the Sun and Venus in the 7th indicate that the querent will have had sexual connection with another woman; Jupiter in the 7th, his own wife; Mercury or the Moon—a prostitute; Saturn, a low caste woman. The age of the woman will be according to the age of the Moon.

If the Moon in the 7th is *bala*, the woman will be a young girl; Mercury also denotes a young girl; Saturn—an elderly lady; Sun or Jupiter—a lady in confinement; Mars and Venus—a quarrelsome woman. Thus should be found out the age of the woman.

NOTES

The question is "which woman I am thinking of to have intimacy with ". Combinations are given in stanzas 35 and 36 for answering such a question.

The Moon is Bala or young till the 5th lunar day, i.e., when his distance from the Sun is 48°. If the same question, is put by a woman the results given above apply to the man. If Saturn is in the 7th, she will have intimacy with an old man, etc.

शुभेत्थशाले हिमगौ चतुष्ट्ये सौख्यातिरेकः सविलासहासः ।
क्रूरेत्थशाले हिरुणौ सरोषे क्रूरान्वितेऽभूत्कलहोनृवध्वाः ॥ ३७ ॥

पीडाऽथवाऽऽसीत्सुरते युवत्या रजो यथाऽस्तर्क्षमुपतितद्द्वत् ।
लग्ने सुरेज्ये भृगुजे कलत्रे तुर्ये हिमांशौ सविलासहासम् ॥ ३८ ॥

Stanzas 37 and 38: When the Moon having Ithasala with benefics is in a Kendra, the querent will enjoy with pleasure and happiness. When the Moon's Ithasala is with a malefic, the couple's union will be marked by quarrels and angry exchanges or the union will result in affliction. The nature of secretion in the woman will be according to the nature of the sign in the 7th house. Jupiter in the ascendant, Venus in the 7th, the Moon in the 4th-the secretion will be to the complete satisfaction and joy of the couple.

शुभग्रहोत्थे च कंबूलयोगे युतो रजः पुष्पसुगन्धयुक्तम् ।
स्वर्क्षोच्चगे हर्म्यरतं निगद्यं स्थिते द्विदेहे वनिता स्वकीया ॥ ३९ ॥

Stanza 39: If the Moon has a Kamboola Yoga with a benefic, the woman's secretion will be fresh like a flower and of pleasant odour. If the Moon is in his own house or exaltation, the union will be in a mansion.

If the Moon is in a common sign, union is with one's own wife.

चरोदये सा रमिते परस्त्री केन्द्रे शनौ सा सुरजा दिवारतिम् ।
निशोदयेऽशे त्रिखगे च रात्रो दिवानिशं
                            तद्द्वलिनोर्द्विखेटयोः ॥ ४० ॥

Stanza 40: If the ascendant is a movable sign, the querent will have sexual intimacy with a woman, not his own wife. When Saturn is in the 4th, the union will be with a woman in menses. When the lord of a diurnal sign is in the 3rd or in the 9th, the union will be during the day. If the lord of a nocturnal sign is in the 3rd or the 9th, the union will be during the night. If both lords are in the 3rd or the 8th, the querent will have union both during day and night.

On Trade And Commerce

मेषे वषे च मिथुने शुभयुक्तदृष्टे न ग्रैष्मिकं तु सुलभं
भविता पृथिव्याम् ।
सूर्ये धनुर्मृगघटेषु च सारधान्यंकुर्यात्समर्धमशुभैः
सहितोऽसमर्धम् ॥ ४१ ॥

Stānza 41: If at the time of query, Aries, Taurus or Gemini rises aspected by or conjoined with benefics, the food crops, pertaining to Greeshma season, will not thrive well. When the ascendant is Sagittarius, Capricorn and Aquarius occupied by the Sun, cereals will be available. If the Sun is aspected by or conjoined with malefics, there will be scarcity.

लग्ने बलाढ्ये निजनाथसौम्यैर्युक्तेक्षिते केन्द्रगतैः शुभैश्च ।
सवैः समर्घं निबलंविलग्ने केन्द्रेषु पापैः सकलं समर्धम् ॥ ४२ ॥

Stanza 42: When the query ascendant is endowed with strength and aspected by or conjoined with the lord of the ascendant or benefic planets and benefics occupy quadrants, moderate trade prices will prevail. Otherwise, high trade prices will rule.

राका कुहू शशिपभास्वदजप्रदेशे लग्नेश्वराः
शुभखगैर्युतवीक्षिताश्चेत् ।
तद्वत्सरे जगति सौख्यमलंप्रकुर्युः पापादिते गदनरेन्द्रभयं
प्रजानाम् ॥ ४३ ॥

Stanza 43: If the lord of the rising sign, at the time of full Moon, new Moon and entry of the Sun and the Moon into Aries, is aspected by on in conjunction with benefics, happiness and peace will prevail in the world. If the lord of Lagna is afflicted, the people will have fear from diseases and rulers.

मेषप्रवेशोदयतः स्वराशिः केन्द्रेषु पापोडुपतीत्थशाले ।
पापग्रहैर्दृष्ट्ययुतेऽथ तस्मिन् वर्षे गदातिः प्रियमन्नमुर्व्याम् ॥ ४४ ॥

Stanza 44: If the ascendant at the time of Suns' entry into Aries happens to be a Kendra from the Janma Rasi of the querent, and is in Ithasala with malefic planets and the Moon and is aspected by or conjoined with malefics, the year in question forebodes ill-health but plenty of food will be available.

भानोर्भेषप्रवेशोदयभवनपतिः सद्ग्रहः स्वोच्चसंस्थः
स्वस्थो वाऽपि केन्द्रे शुभगगनचरैर्दृष्ट्ययुक्तो बलाढ्यः ।
तस्मिन्वर्षे विदध्याज्जगांत शुभसुखं भूरिसस्यं सुवृद्धिः
क्रूरः क्रूरादितो वा दिशति नृपभयं कष्टमन्नं महर्धम् ॥ ४५ ॥

Stanza 45: If the lord of the ascendant at the time of solar ingress into Aries being a benefic planct, occupies his own or exaltation place or a Kendra and is aspected by or in conjunction with benefics and is endowed with strength, then during that year, the world will witness happiness, crops will thrive well and there will be plenty in the land. When the ascendant lord is a malefic, weak and afflicted, there will be fear from rulers, famine and food prices will soar.

NOTES

The above stanzas deal with mundane astrology. I do not propose to elaborate the combinations given. in stanzas 41 to 45 as they are clear and I propose writing a separate book exclusively devoted to this subject.

Individual's Future

जन्मोदयाद्धास्वबजप्रवेशलग्नं हि यद्धावगतं शुभान्वितम् ।
तद्धाववृद्धि विदधाति तस्मिन् वर्षे नृणां पापयुतं
तदन्यथा ॥ ४६ ॥

Stanza 46: That Bhava in the birth horoscope, in which the ascendant at the time of Sun's ingress into Aries falls, will prosper well during the year ahead provided it is occupied by or conjoined with benefic planets. Otherwise the contrary will be the result.

NOTES

A principle is given here to estimate how the year ahead will be for a person, on the basis of the commencement of the solar year. If the Lagna rising when the Sun enters Aries is Gemini and this happens to be the 4th house in a person's horoscope, the prospects of the 4th house will progress provided it is not afflicted in the solar ingress chart. We can only estimate approximate results and the relevance of this method in a work on Horary Astrology is not quite clear.

जन्मोदये देहसुखं धनेऽर्थलाभस्तृतीये च कुटुम्बवृद्धिः ।
तुर्ये सुहृत्सौख्यमात्मजाप्तिः पुत्रेऽथ षष्ठेऽरिपराजयः
स्यात् ॥ ४७ ॥

स्त्रीसौख्याप्तिर्भवति मदने मृत्युरुग्भीश्च रन्ध्रे
धर्मार्थांतिस्तपसि दशमे वित्तसौख्यास्पदाप्तिः ।
लाभे लाभः सुखधनचयो दुःखदारिद्र्यमन्त्ये
पुंसो मेषे प्रविशति रवौ जन्मलग्नाद्द्विलग्ने ॥ ४८ ॥

Stanzas 47 and 48: When the rising sign in the solar ingress chart which is endowed with strength falls in different places in a person's horoscope, the following results will happen: In the first house, body comforts and physical happiness; 2nd, gain of money or increase of wealth; 3rd, happiness in the family; 4th, pleasant relations with friends; 5th, birth of children ; 6th, defeat of enemies; 7th, happiness from women ; 8th, danger of death and disease ; 9th, inclination to righteous deeds; 10th, mental peace and gain of a position ; 11th, all kinds of gains ; and 12th, sorrow and poverty.

On Tajaka Aspects

नवपञ्चमयोर्दृष्टिः पादोना सर्वदृष्टिः सबला ।
मेलापकदृष्टिरियं प्रत्यक्षस्नेहदृष्टिरिति ॥ ४९ ॥

Stanza 49: The 5th and the 9th aspect is 75% strong. It is the strongest and the most beneficial of all aspects and is openly friendly.

तृतीयैकादशयोर्दृष्टौ यो वीक्षते तृतीयदृशा ।
तद्दृष्टिस्त्र्यंशोना नान्यत्र तु षड्भागदृष्टिश्च ॥ ५० ॥

अनयोर्गूप्तस्नेहा दृष्टिः सर्वत्र कार्यसिद्धिकरी ।
दशमचतुर्थजदृष्टिः पादोना दुर्जना ख्याता ॥ ५१ ॥

Stanzas 50 and 51: Of the 3rd and 11th aspect, the aspect on the 3rd is 40% strong; on the 11th it is 10%; the

3rd and 11th aspect is secretly friendly and is always favourable for fulfilment of desires. The 4th and 10th aspect is also 75% strong. It is an unfavourable and unfriendly aspect. The 1st and 4th aspect is 100% strong. It is secretly hostile and unfavourable.

NOTES

Stanzas 49 to 51 deal with aspects according to Tajaka theory. The following aspects are considered:

Trine:—When two planets are 120° apart, i.e., in the 5th and the 9th from each other, it is 75% full, the strongest and the most benefic of all aspects and denotes fulfilment.

Sextile:—When two planets are in the 3rd and the 11th from each other (60° apart) this aspect is caused. The aspect on the 3rd is 40% strong, and the aspect on the 11th is 10% strong. This is a beneficial aspect giving rise to the same result as the trine.

Square aspect:—When two planets are in the 4th and the 10th from each other (90° apart) a square aspect is formed. It is 45% strong. It is an inimical aspect always indicating difficulties, obstruction, etc.

Opposition:—When two planets are in the 7th from each other (180°), this aspect arises. This is a 100% strong aspect and always gives rise to unfavourable and adverse results.

In delineating the results of the square and opposition as always adverse, the inherent nature of the planets seems to have been ignored by the Tajaka writers. It occurs to me that the nature of the planet can influence to some extent the nature of the aspect. For instance, a square or an opposition between Jupiter and Venus cannot be as adverse as that between Mars and Saturn. However, in interpreting Prasna charts, this aspect is not taken into account for reasons best known to Tajaka writers.

सर्वाश्चैता हि दृशो द्वादशभागान्तरे भवेयुश्चेत् ।
सर्वविशेषः प्रोक्तो दृष्ट्यनुसारात्फलं चिन्त्यम् ॥ ५२ ॥
सूर्यः पञ्चदशांशैरिन्दुर्द्वादशभिरवनिजोऽष्टाभिः ।
सप्तांशैर्वुधशुक्रौ गुरुमन्दौ नवभिरीक्षेते ॥ ५३ ॥

Stanzas 52 and 53: Though the orb in respect of all aspects is 12° the results should be interpreted on the basis of special orbs with reference to each planet, viz., the Sun 15°, the Moon 12°, Mars 8°, Mercury 7°, Jupiter 9°, Venus 7° and Saturn 9°.

NOTES

The general orb of aspect is 12°, i.e., 6° on either side of the exact situation of the planet. But the intensity of the aspect and the intensity of the result depend upon the special orbs or deepthamsas as given in stanza 53.

यदि शीघ्रः स्वल्पांशः पश्चान्मन्दं घनांशमुपगम्य ।
स्वदीप्तभागमस्मै दत्ते ध्रुवमित्थशालयोगोऽयम् ॥ ५४ ।

Ithasala Yoga

लिप्तार्धविलिप्तिकाभ्यां यदि होनो मन्दतोऽप्यतुल्यः स्यात् ।
तत्पूर्णमित्थशालं मुथशिलमपि तथ्यते तज्ज्ञैः ॥ ५५ ॥

Stanzas 54 and 55: If a faster planet with less longitude is backwards of a slower planet with a greater longitude, Ithasala Yoga is caused. If the latter planet is ahead of the former by a minute or 30", it is a complete Ithasala. This Yoga becomes Muthaseela.

NOTES

These Tajaka Yogas have been elaborated in the latest edition of my book *Varshaphal* or *The Hindu Progressed Horoscope* and the esteemed reader will do well to study this book. I shall however give a brief explanation in these pages.

Saturn is the slowest moving planet and the Moon the fastest. The speed becomes faster in the order of Saturn, Jupiter, Mars, the Sun, Venus, Mercury and the Moon.

Take the given chart. According to stanza 54, the Sun a faster-moving planet having lesser longitude is backwards of Mars the slower-moving planet in greater longitude. For an exact square aspect to occur, the difference is 14° and this falls within the Deepthamsa (orb of the aspect). Hence Ithasala Yoga is present. In other words, it is an applying aspect here.

	Chart No. 1		
			Sun 2
	Lagna Mars 16		

When the aspecting bodies are within a degree of the exact aspect or in exact aspect, it is a Poorna or complete Yoga. Ithasala Yoga is also known as Muthaseela.

Easarapha Yoga

अथ शीघ्रो मन्टगतैरपि भागेकं समुत्तरत्यग्रे ।
तदिहेसराफसंज्ञो मूसरिफः कथ्यतेऽत्यशुभः ॥ ५६ ॥

Stanza 56: When a faster-moving planet is ahead of a slower-moving planet by one degree, Easarapha is caused. It is also called Musaripha. This is an unfavourable combination.

NOTES

The faster-moving planet (*e.g.*, Mercury) should be ahead of the slower-moving planet (*e.g.*, Venus) by 1°, *i.e.*, it is a separating aspect and connotes that results will be unfavourable. If suppose the faster-moving planet (*e.g.*, Mercury) is backwards of the slower-moving planet (*e.g.*, Venus) by one degree, the process in stanza 56 is reversed. Then you have an applying aspect and it is Ithasala. In other words—Musaripha is also Ithasala when the aspect is separating.

Naktha Yoga

यद्युभयदृष्टिरहितो यद्दन्यः शीघ्रगोऽन्तरे भूत्वा ।
पश्चाच्च तदन्यस्मै ददाति तेजः स नक्तसंज्ञः स्यात् ॥ ५७ ॥

Stanza 57: When there is no mutual aspect between two planets but a faster (than the two not in aspect) planet is in between in aspect with both then this faster-moving planet transfers light from the (other faster) planet to slower one. This is Nakta Yoga.

NOTES

Take the chart given below. There is no aspect between Jupiter and Mercury. A faster-moving planet Moon is in aspect with both Mercury and Jupiter. Hence it transfers the light from Mercury to other planet Jupiter slower. Under such an aspect, a third person's help will be sought for settlement of issues, etc.

Jupiter 12			
	Navamsa I		
			Mercury 10
Moon 8			Lagna

EXAMPLES

स्त्रीलाभस्य प्रश्ने कन्यालग्ने बुध: पति: सिंहे ।
मीने च तत्पतिर्गुरुस्तत्रानयोर्नत्वस्ति दृष्टिस्तु ॥ ५८ ॥

शीघ्रश्चन्द्रो द्वाभ्यां दृष्टो बुधोत्तन्महो नीत्वा ।
जीवाय ददौ तद्वस्परहस्ताद्योषित: प्राप्ति: ॥ ५९ ॥

Stanzas 58 and 59: In regard to a question about getting a wife: the Ascendant is Virgo and the lord Mercury is in Leo. The lord of the 7th Jupiter is in the 7th. There is no aspect between these two planets. The faster-moving planet is placed between Mercury and Jupiter and in aspect with them transfers light from Mercury to Jupiter. The bride will be secured through the assistance of another person.

Yamaya Yoga

अथ यदि मन्दोऽन्तःस्थो द्वावपि पश्यति निजोक्तदीप्तदृशा ।
तेजो नीत्वा शीघ्राद्ददाति मन्दाय तद्यमया ॥ ६० ॥

Stanza 60: When there is no aspect between two lords and a slower-moving planet is in between these two lords involved in aspect with them, then the slower-moving planet will transfer light from the other faster of the two lords to the slower. This is Yamaya Yoga.

	Venus 16	
	Navamsa 11	Jupiter 10
	Lagna	Moon 8

NOTES

In the chart given there is no aspect between Venus (lord of Lagna) and the Moon (lord of the 10th. Jupiter is in Cancer in aspect with both Vens and the Moon. He transfers 'light' from the faster-moving Moon to the slower-moving Venus. Hence this is Yamaya Yoga.

Kamboola Yoga

उभयेत्थशालयोगे यदि चन्द्रोऽप्यत्र मुथशिलविधायी ।
तत्कम्बूलं हि भवेदुत्तममध्याधमैर्भेदैः ॥ ६१ ॥

Miscellaneous Matters

Stanza 61: When there is Ithasala between two planets and the Moon is also involved in Ithasala with one of the planets, the resulting Yoga is Kamboola. There are three varieties of this yoga, *viz.*, exalted, mediocre and debilitated.

Thus ends Neelakanta's *Prasna Tantra*.

NOTES

When two planets are in Ithasala and the Moon is in Ithasala with either of them, Kamboola Yoga is caused. It is *par excellence*, medium or ordinary according to the strength the Moon and the other two planets become endowed with.

In the example chart, Jupiter and Venus åre in Ithasala. The Moon is also in Ithasala with both.

Therefore, Kamboola Yoga is caused. Jupiter and Venus are both exalted. And hence it is a *par excellence* Kamboola.

Venus 12			
			Jupiter 14
Moon 10			

In Kamboola Yoga three planets are involved, *viz.*, the lord of Lagna, the lord of event (significator) and the Moon. When the two lords and the Moon are exalted or in their own houses, it is *Uttamottama*. When the Moon is exalted and the other two planets are in their own Navamsa, Drekkana, Hadda, etc., it is *Madhyamottama*. When the Moon is not exalted, but the other lords are in own Navamsas, Drekkanas, etc., it is *Uttama*. When the Moon is exalted or occupies own house and the other two lords are debilitated, etc, it is *Uttamadhama*. When the Moon is in its own Navamsa and Dwadasamsa and the other two planets are in their own or exalted places, it is *Madhyamottama*. It is *Madhyama* if the Moon is in his own Navamsa or Drekkana and is in Ithasala with the lord of Lagna in own house or *Hadda*. It will be *Adhama* if none of the three planets have *panchadhikara* (See Chapter III of *Varshaphal*). Thus the benefic, more benefic or most benefic nature of the Kamboola Yoga should be ascertained on the basis of the inherent strength of the Moon and other planets.

With the description of some of these important Yogas, Neelakantha's *Prasna Tantra* ends.

OM TAT SAT.

Some Examples

I am giving 12 examples chosen from the innumerable number of horary questions answered by me. They will illustrate some of the important principles.

Horary astrology comes in handy for answering any type of questions whether or not one knows his or her birth details. Each house signifies certain events but the student of astrology alone should be able to assign through experience, the innumerable events of today to appropriate houses. If a question such as "Whether it would be safe to travel by air" is put, one has to adapt the ancient tool to suit the modern conditions of travel. If it is a long trip, say overseas, take the 9th house. If it is a trip within the country, take the 3rd house; and if it is within one's own state, say a local trip, take the 12th house as the significator. Sometimes, the 7th house also gives clues for predicting a foreign trip provided the lord of the 9th is in the 7th.

Basic formulas are provided by ancient texts which can be considered common to all charts but interpretative methods become varied in view of the changed political, economic, transport and other conditions.

It is always best to frame the question in a clear manner, e.g., "Will I marry?" And as a matter of corollary, the subsidiary question-when, will automatically arise. With slight modifications, the house in a horary chart signify more or less the same events as in a natal chart and by a consideration of the relative dispositions, strength, afflictions etc, of the significators; any type of question can be answered successfully. Here again the judgment will have to rest on interpretative ability or intuition of the astrologer.

The reader will do well to study the following charts in the light of the above general remarks.

I. Any Likelihood of Becoming Rich?

Data: 20-10-1950 at 9 p.m. (I.S.T.) at Bangalore.

Rahu 4.57		Ascdt. 25.32	
X 15-27 Jupiter 5-56 Moon 5-23			
	Mars 25.31	Sun 5-0	Kethu 4-57 Saturn 5.6 Mercury 26.57 Venus 28.45

The querent, a petty shop-keeper, was anxious to know whether he would ever become rich.

Lords of the ascendant and the 2nd are in conjunction. The lord of the 2nd is exalted in the 5th. The second is aspected by Mars, lord of the 12th. From Chandra Lagna, the lord of the second is in Lagna.

These factors denote the querent would become well-to-do.

How would he become rich? The ascendant lord has Ithasala with the lord of the 2nd in the 5th. The means would be that signified by the 5th house, *viz.*, speculation, brokerage, etc. Lord of the 7th Mars (partner, wife, etc.) is also in Ithasala with the lords of the ascendant and the 2nd. There is also Yamya Yoga between the lords of the 11th (Jupiter) and 2nd. Consequently, it was predicted that through marriage he would get some financial assistance and with this capital he would do business and become fairly well-to-do. Mercury and Venus being 2° apart these signified about 2 years.

He was married within a year and with the small dowry he got he did commission agency business by arranging for sale of houses, estates, etc., and became fairly rich.

II. Mother's Longevity

The ascendant (querent) is Virgo occupied by Mars and Kethu typifying the anxiety of the querent. Lord of the ascendant is in Ithasala with Jupiter lord of the 4th while the sigificators (querent—Mercury and mother—Jupiter) are in conjunction confirming the query is about the mother.

From the 4th, the 8th represents mother's longevity. It is occupied by its own lord Moon and the lords of the 4th and 8th therefrom are in Ithasala (applying). The Moon is equally well placed. The 4th house is not vitiated by the lords of the 6th and 8th therefrom

Data: 1-3-1950 at 8 p.m. (I.S.T.) at Bangalore.

Rahu 17-36			X 12-40
Sun 18-43			Moon 11-43
Jupiter 28-43 Mercury 28-20 Venus 12-50			Saturn (R) 24-47
			Lagna 12-8 Mars 17-25 Kethu 17-36

but the 4th lord and the 6th lord therefrom are in conjunction (applying). Consequently, the illness would be in progress until the exact conjunction was over (by 24th March 1950). The lord of the 4th though debilitated has attained Neechabhanga. The prediction was given that there was no fear for the life of the querent's mother and that she would live for many years.

The lady who was 45 then died in 1965 when she completed 60 years.

III. Getting A Child

Data: 9-9-1947 at 12-25 p.m. (I.S.T.) at Bangalore.

		Rahu 4-16	Moon 8-46 Mars 25-12
			Saturn 25-4
			Sun 24-5 X 26-5 Venus 25-36
Mandi 7-41	Ascdt. 22-52 Jupiter 0-16 Kethu 4-16		Mercury 3-52

The querent wanted to know whether he would get an issue from his wife. The couple had no children during eight years of married life.

Lagna (Scorpio) and the lord (Mars) represent the querent. The 5th house (Pisces) and the lord of the 5th (Jupiter) are significators. The Moon may also be considered as signifying the querent. Neither the Moon nor the lord of the ascendant is in the 5th. The lord of the 5th is not in the ascendant. These are not favourable for getting children. But the lord of the ascendant Mars is in favourable Ithasala (trine) with the lord of the 5th Jupiter. This is a fine combination. There is also Ithasala (sextile) between the lords of the 5th and the 11th. Hence balancing these two factors, it was predicted that the querent would have a daughter (Lagna and the 5th are even signs) after an abortion

(Mars in unfavourable Muthasila to 5th). The Lagna has passed 6 navamsas (equivalent to 6 months) and 2° 52' (equivalent to 25 days) in the 7th navamsa, Adapting the principle given in stanza 36, Chapter II (page 45), it was predicted that she might conceive by about 5th or 6th April 1948, i.e., 6 months and 26 days from the date of question. It was subsequently found that the timing was not quite correct. In fact she was said to have conceived on the 1st or 2nd of July 1948. It will be seen that Mars (lord of the ascendant in the Prasna chart) was transiting Jupiter's position in the Prasna chart.

IV. Is the Absent Person Alive or Dead?

Data: 1-7-1942 at 8-15 p.m. (I.S.T.) at Bombay.

		Venus 12-55 Saturn 13-12 Mercury 27-20	Jupiter 13-15 Sun 17-33
Kethu 15-40 Moon 0-41			Mars 19-12
Ascdt. 9-13			Rahu 15-40
		X 18-40	

The query was about the querent's son. All of a sudden he had left home and his whereabouts had not been known.

Some Examples

The lord of the ascendant Saturn is in the 5th suggesting that the query relates to the 5th house. The significators are the 5th house and 5th lord (Venus). The 8th from the 5th is unafflicted but associated with the lord of the 8th. The significator (Venus) has no evil aspects with any malefic lord. The lord of Lagna is no doubt conjoined with the lord of the 6th but the conjunction is separating.

The evidence is all in favour of the absent person not being dead. But what about his whereabouts and when was he likely to return?

Here the 5th signifies the absent person, the 11th rules the 'way' and the 8th his happiness, etc., Lord of the 8th (4th from the 5th) Sun in the 2nd (from the 5th) with the lord of the 8th (from the 5th) Jupiter indicate that the absent person was not quite happy due to financial troubles, and that he might be in hiding as the 7th from the 5th happens to be Scorpio.

The Lagna is Chara (moveable) and lord of the 7th Moon is in the ascendant. The lord of the 5th is conjoining the lord of the ascendant and is in Ithasala (applying) with the lord of the 11th. These signify his return home. Venus conjoined Saturn on 4th July and the Ithasala aspect between Venus and Mars became exact on 13th July. It was predicted that the whereabouts of the boy would be known about 4th July and that he would return by 13th July.

Actually the whereabouts were not known but he returned of his own accord on 12th July 1942.

V. Illness

Data: 27-5-1964 at 6-20 a.m. (I.S.T.) at New Delhi.

	Mars 22-32 Mercury 19-00 Jupiter 18-40	Ascdt. 19-19 Sun 14-5	Rahu 11-39 Venus 14-51
Saturn 12-50 X 2-42	22-21		
Kethu 11-39	Moon 20-48		

According to *Prasna Tantra*, the ascendant signifies the physician, the 7th signifies the disease or illness, the 10th denotes the patient and the 4th the treatment. But in my experience, the 6th house should have greater weight than the 7th house so far as the disease is concerned.

Venus, lord of the ascendant (who also happens to be lord of the 6th) is in the 2nd in Ithasala with Saturn, Mars, Mercury (malefics) and Jupiter. Venus is in conjunction with Rahu. The Ithasala Yoga from lord of the 8th Jupiter is applying. With malefic Saturn also the Yoga is applying. The seat of disease is in the face—partial paralysis. Jupiter's aspect as lord of the 8th favours gradual relief. Lord of the ascendant in the 8th from the Moon is no sign of early recovery.

As the ascendant is a fixed sign the suspected disease (*viz.*, partial paralysis) is correct.

As the indicator of disease (Venus) is with Rahu no hope could be given for early cure of the disease which might have originated from an intemperate sexual life.

The Moon in the 7th in adverse aspect with Saturn in the 10th is not favourable for recovery. Jupiter lord of the 8th has no adverse aspect with Venus lord of the ascendant, and the 6th, but is in conjunction with Mars, lord of the 7th and the 12th. Further aggravation is indicated but no early death.

The house of patient, *viz.*, the 10th is occupied by Saturn. The house of treatment' is aspected by Saturn and the lord of the 4th is in malefic Ithasala with Saturn. Consequently, the prescription of medicine will not be quite appropriate and the patient would continue to linger on with the disease.

As the Sun rules the fourth, herbs mantras, precious stones, etc., ruled by the Sun could give some relief to the patient. The patient who is still living continues to suffer from the same disease. He is unable to speak but is able to move about a little.

VI. Marriage

The querent aged about 30 wanted to know whether he would marry. The querent's significator (ascendant lord) is Jupiter. The significator of the marriage is Mercury (lord of the 7th).

The significators (Jupiter and Mercury) are in Ithasala. And the ascendant lord and the Moon are

Data: 6-11-1962 at 9-20 a.m. (I.S.T.) at Bangalore.

Jupiter 11-11 Moon 2-20			Rahu 14-54 Mars 20-20
Saturn 13-29 Kethu 11-45	R-3		
Ascdt. 8-0	Venus 1-52	Mercury 9-50 Sun 21-12	X 14-51

also in conjunction. Therefore, the testimony for marriage could be considered to be favourable. But the 7th lord Mercury is in combustion and the 8th house is afflicted. This means obstructions. Mars and Saturn occupying the 8th and 2nd respectively are also in Ithasala with the lord of the 7th. Therefore, attempts will be made by family members to prevent marriage. However, the Moon's involvement in Ithasala with both the significators and the ascendant lord giving rise to Kamboola Yoga favours marriage after initial hurdles.

The exact aspect between the significator and the ascendant lord will be formed within a day. And of course marriage could not be predicted within this period. The Moon also as significator (because of his being lord of the 8th and causing Ithasala with the lord of the 7th) is 9° behind the ascendant lord. But

Aquarius being a fixed sign it was predicted that the marriage was likely within 9 months-March 1963 when transit Mercury conjoined Jupiter in the chart.

Mercury the significator is conjoined with the Sun. The bride will be fair, honest (Jupiter's aspect), restless and somewhat domineering (Mars' aspect), industrious (Saturn's aspect) and hailing from a fairly well-to-do family

The marriage took place in March 1963.

VII. End of a Strike

Data: 2-9-1968 at 2-10 p.m. (I.S.T.) at Madras.

Rahu 19-00	Saturn (R) 3-00		
			Mars 25-42
			Sun 17-58 Jupiter 22-57
Ascendant 14-00 Moon 19-25			X 21-00 Venus 8-6 Mercury 8-57 Kethu 19-00

The query was put by trunk-telephone by the Editor of a leading Newspaper about the end of the workers' strike.

The Lagna represents the querent. Since the strike is in the nature of a dispute, the 7th house signifies the strike. Lord of the ascendant is in the 9th strongly placed with the lord of the 9th. The Moon is beneficially disposed in the ascendant. The Moon is in Ithasala (forming) with Jupiter the ascendant lord and with the Sun lord of the 9th (separating), in Ithasala (applying) with Jupiter. The Sun lord of the 9th is in the 9th. There is no affliction to the ascendant lord.

Mercury the significator of the "strikers" is exalted in the 10th but is in Ithasala with Venus (lord of the 12th from the 7th) and Kethu. While the opposition is strong, it cannot last long.

Lord of the ascendant is ahead of the Sun lord of the 9th by about 5 degrees. It was predicted that without the management having to yield much, the strike would end by about 5 weeks' time.

The prediction was verified with a time lag of a few days.

VIII. Recovery Of Stolen Property

The 1st (Aries) and its lord (Mars) are the significators of the querent. The 7th (Libra) and its lord (Venus) are the significators of the thief. The 4th (Cancer) and its lord (the Moon) are the significators of the property.

Lord of the 4th Moon is in conjunction with Venus lord of the 2nd (money). The Moon represents precious stones. Venus represents diamonds. It was surmised that precious stones, especially diamonds, must have been stolen.

Some Examples

Data: 14-3-1942 at 8-15 a.m. (I.S.T.) Lat. 13° N., Long. 5h. 40m. 20s. E.

Sun 1-17	Ascendant 2-21	Saturn 2-14 Mars 12-20 Jupiter 21-56	
Kethu 21-32 Mercury 4-50			
Moon 25-46 Venus 20-00			Rahu 21-32
X 26-43			

The 7th is not occupied. But the 7th house is in Ithasala with Mercury lord of the 3rd (neighbour) and 6th (enemy). Lord of the 7th Venus (female planet) is with the Moon (female planet). The thief must be a handsome lady belonging to a neighbourhood inimically disposed towards the querent.

Lord of the 4th Moon is in 11th house. Lord of the 2nd (Venus) is in Muthasila with the lord of the 9th (Jupiter). Recovery was predicted.

The Moon (significator of property) is heading for a conjunction with the 11th house (30° Aquarius) and the conjunction takes place on 17-3-1942. Lords of the 2nd and 9th are in Ithasala. The significator Moon is in a Chara Rasi and is heading towards Ithasala (square) with Saturn. It was predicted that the property would be recovered within about 6 days' time.

As predicted, the diamond ring was recovered. The young daughter of a farmer friend lifted it from the bedroom of the querent's wife. Through the intercession of mutual friends, it was restored back to the querent on the 5th day.

IX. Outcome of a Law Suit

Data: 1-12-1963 at 10-15 a.m. (I.S.T.) at Bangalore.

Jupiter 17-39		Moon 19-12	Rahu 21-5
Saturn 25-53 Ascendant 19-36	21-30		
Mercury 0-40 Mars 5-31 Venus 10-2 Kethu 21-5	Sun 16-21		

The querent who had filed a suit against his debtor wanted to know the outcome of the action.

The ascendant Capricorn and the lord Saturn signify the planitiff, the 7th house (Cancer) and the lord of the 7th Moon signify the defendant.

The lords of the ascendant and the 7th are in Ithasala indicating that the parties will agree. Lord of the ascendant is in the ascendant. The plaintiff's case is strong. Lord of the 7th is exalted in the 11th from the 7th. The defence is equally strong. But four planets are in the 12th from the ascendant denoting "weakness" of the plaintiff's position. But the Sun in the 11th does not favour his losing the case. The defendant's planetary positions are more favourable because there are no planets in the 6th (12th from the 7th). On the contrary, the 11th (from the 7th) is well fortified. In between the plaintiff (Saturn) and the defendant (Moon) Jupiter is in his own house. Jupiter signifies 'Judges'. Therefore, it was predicted that there would be compromise due to the good offices of the Judge himself but with a little disadvantage to the plaintiff and that since the ascendant and the 7th are moveable signs, the compromise would be effected very soon.

As indicated, after 6 months, the parties compromised.

X. Foreign Travel

The querent, a Professor in an Educational Institute, desired to know whether a foreign trip he was contemplating would come off early.

Lord of the ascendant, Mars, is in the ascendant and has no aspect with the lord of the 9th who is placed in the 6th. But the 9th house is in Ithasala with the lord of the 1st. Lord of the 9th is also not in aspect with any planet.

Data: 1-3-1957 at 10-25 a.m. (I.S.T.) at Bangalore.

	Ascendant 24-40 Mars 27-45	Ketu 1-47	
Sun 18-33 Moon 13-25 Mercury 2-47 Venus 7-23	RASI R-26		
X 15-47			
	Rahu 1-47 Saturn 22-45		Jupiter 7-9

From the Moon, the lord of the ascendant is placed in a quadrant. There is a hostile Muthasila between Saturn (lord of Chandra Lagna) and Venus, lord of the 9th.

It was predicted that the foreign journey would not materialise in the near future, but might be possible when Jupiter transited Sagittarius forming a favourable Muthasila with Mars lord of Prasna Lagna, i.e., about January 1961. The prediction was fulfilled.

XI. Leaving the Present Job

Lord of the ascendant Saturn is in Ithasala with the lord of the 12th (Jupiter) and the lord of the 11th (Mars), in the 9th. This indicates the querent will change over to a new "employer". The lord of the

Some Examples

Data: 10-12-1968 at 10-25 a.m. (I.S.T.) at Bangalore.

Saturn (R) 26-50 Rahu 13-48			
	RASI 29-71		Moon 23-37
Ascendant 21-51 Venus 8-20			
	X 0-42 Mercury 27-57 Sun 26-13		Jupiter 11-29 Ketu 13-48 Mars 26-33

ascendant is again in the 3rd in a common sign. There is only a change of employment and no change of place. The Moon and Jupiter aspect the ascendant and the 7th is occupied by its own lord. The new employer will take kindly to the querent.

The strongest indication for change is the Ithasala between the ascendant lord and the lord of the 9th in the 11th and the Ithasala between the ascendant lord and the lord of the 12th in the 9th.

Lords of the 10th and the 12th are in Ithasala, hence the job will be changed. The distance between the 10th lord and the 12th lord is 246°. Consequently, the change would occur by about 8 months' time.

At the time of writing this, the querent is about to leave the job and seek another one.

XII. Profession

Data: 5-5-1949 at 2 p.m. (I.S.T.) at Bangalore.

	Rahu 3-11 Sun 22-50 Mars 12-3 Venus 27-36	X 18-00 Mercury 13-00	
	RASI R-3		Moon 15-23
Jupiter 10-6			Ascendant 16-40 Saturn 7-27
		Kethu 3-11	

The querent wanted to know about preferment in profession. The significators to be considered are the lords of the ascendant (the Sun) and the 10th (Venus). The lord of the ascendant is in Ithasala not only with the lord of the 10th Venus but also with the lord of the 9th, Mars, a Yogakaraka. These two lords are in hostile Ithasala with Jupiter. Consequently a preferment could be expected after putting forth much effort. The difficulty is emphasised by the Ithasala between the planet in the 10th and Saturn lord of the 7th in the ascendant. Saturn's position indicates that there is opposition for the querent to get the desired preferment. The applying Ithasala between the Moon and the lord of the 10th and between the Moon and the ascendant lord denotes that he will get a new assignment, consistent with strong disposition of the 10th house, the 10th lord and the planet in the 10th. All these indicated that the querent would get a new and worthy position. The distance between the Sun and Venus being about 5°, it was predicted that the indicated event would materialise by about October 1949. The querent who had previously held the post of an Assistant Manager in a business concern became a Manager in another leading firm during October 1949.

Index of Technical Terms

Amla	— Sour
Apoklima	— 3rd, 6th, 9th, and 12th houses.
Asta	— Conjunction with the Sun, Combustion
Avastha	— State or condition of a planet
Beeja Sphuta	— Point of fertility in the male
Bhattotpala	— A commentator of *Brihat Jataka*
Bhavas	— Houses
Bhavishya Ithasala	— Applying aspect.
Bhuvana Deepika	— A Treatise on Horary Astrology
Brahmins	— The spiritual caste
Brahma	— Creator, the first of Hindu Trinity
Brihat Jataka	— A great classic in Astrology
Chara Rasi	— Moveable signs
Daiva	— Unknown factor
Daivagnya	— Astrologer

Index of Technical Terms 215

Dasama	— 10th House
Deena	— Fallen or debilitation
Deeptha	— Blazing or exaltation
Devi	— Goddess
Dhanakaraka	— Indicator of wealth, Jupiter
Dhatu	— Mineral
Dhurdhura Yoga	— Planets on either side of the Moon
Dhruvanadi	— A classic on Nadi Astrology by Satyacharya
Drekkana	— $1/3^{rd}$ Division of a sign
Drishyardha	— The visible hemisphere
Durga	— Goddess of Destruction
Dwadasamsa	— 1/12th Division of a sign
Dwipada Rasi	— Common sign
Easarpha	— A special combination in Tajaka System
Gairikamboola Yoga	— A special combination in Tajaka System
Greeshma	— June and July months
Heena	— Mean
Hora	— Half sign, an hour
Ithasala	— A special combination in Tajaka System.

Japa	— Recitation of a divine name
Jatakarnava	— An ancient astrological work
Jeeva	— Life, spirit
Karakatwas	— Significations
Karma	— Action, also implies deeds done in previous births
Karyapa or Karyesa	— Significator
Karyasiddhi	— Success
Katuka	— Bitter
Kendra	— Quadrant; 1st. 4th, 7th and 10th houses
Khara	— Pungent
Krishneeya	— A classical astrological work
Kshatriya	— Warrior caste
Kshetra Sphuta	— Point of fertility in a female
Kulata	— A fallen woman
Lagna	— Ascendant
Lavana	— Salt
Madhura	— Sweet
Mantras	— Regulated forms of sound vibrations

Index of Technical Terms

Manuja	— Man
Misra	— Mixed
Moola	— Mineral
Mrityu Yoga	— Combination for death
Mudhita	— Friendly place
Musaripha Yoga	— A special combination in Tajaka System
Mushita	— Combust
Nakta Yoga	— A special combination in Tajaka System
Navamsa	— 1/9th division of a sign
Nipeeditha	— Vanquished in war
Panchangas	— Almanacs
Parasari	— System of Astrology propounded by sage Parasara
Prasna Deepika	— A treatise in Horary Astrology
Prasna	— Query
Prasna Chinthamani	— A classical work on Horary Astrology
Prerana	— Prompting
Prushtodaya	— Signs rising by their hinder part.
Punya Saham	— Signification of ruling religion

Rasa	— Taste, Juice, flavour
Sakini	— A female deity
Sarat	— October and November
Sati	— A virtuous wife
Shatpanchasika	— A classical work on Horary Astrology
Shodasa Vargas	— Sixteen kinds of divisions of a sign
Sirshodaya	— Signs rising by head
Sisira	— March and April months
Siva	— The destroyer, the third in Hindu Trinity
Square	— 90 degrees aspect
Sukla Paksha	— Waxing Moon
Sudra	— Agriculture caste
Suveerya	— Gaining vitality
Suptha	— Inimical sign
Swagotradevi	— One's family deity
Swastha	— Own sign
Tajaka	— A system of astrology
Trikona	— Trine, 1st, 5th and 9th house
Upachaya	— 3rd, 6th, 10th and 11th house
Utpala	— An astrological writer and commentator of the 8th Century A.D.

Index of Technical Terms

Vaisya	— Business or Trade caste
Vana Rasi	— Sign governing forests
Varahamihira	— An astrological writer of the 1st Century A.D.
Vargottama	— Similar Rasi and Navamsa positions
Varshaphal	— Annual Results
Vishnu	— Protector, the second of the Hindu Trinity.